REVISE EDEXCEL GCSE (9–1)

History

RUSSIA AND THE SOVIET UNION, 1917–41

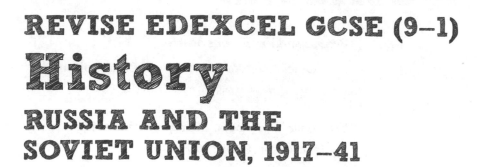

REVISION
GUIDE AND WORKBOOK

Series Consultant: Harry Smith

Author: Rob Bircher

A note from the publisher

In order to ensure that this resource offers high-quality support for the associated Pearson qualification, it has been through a review process by the awarding body. This process confirms that this resource fully covers the teaching and learning content of the specification or part of a specification at which it is aimed. It also confirms that it demonstrates an appropriate balance between the development of subject skills, knowledge and understanding, in addition to preparation for assessment.

Endorsement does not cover any guidance on assessment activities or processes (e.g. practice questions or advice on how to answer assessment questions) included in the resource, nor does it prescribe any particular approach to the teaching or delivery of a related course.

While the publishers have made every attempt to ensure that advice on the qualification and its assessment is accurate, the official specification and associated assessment guidance materials are the only authoritative source of information and should always be referred to for definitive guidance.

Pearson examiners have not contributed to any sections in this resource relevant to examination papers for which they have responsibility.

Examiners will not use endorsed resources as a source of material for any assessment set by Pearson.

Endorsement of a resource does not mean that the resource is required to achieve this Pearson qualification, nor does it mean that it is the only suitable material available to support the qualification, and any resource lists produced by the awarding body shall include this and other appropriate resources.

For the full range of Pearson revision titles across KS2, KS3, GCSE, Functional Skills, AS/A Level and BTEC visit:
www.pearsonschools.co.uk/revise

Pearson

Contents

. . . .

A small bit of small print

Edexcel publishes Sample Assessment Material and the Specification on its website. This is the official content and this book should be used in conjunction with it. The questions in Now try this have been written to help you practise every topic in the book. Remember: the real exam questions may not look like this.

Threats to the tsarist regime

By 1917, peasants, town workers and the urban middle classes were discontented with the way that Russia was governed by the tsarist **regime** (authoritarian rule).

DISCONTENTED		SUPPORTIVE
Peasants (wanted more land)		The army
Workers (wanted better conditions)	**THE TSARIST REGIME**	The Okhrana (secret police)
Liberals (wanted more political freedoms)		Conservatives
Nationalities (wanted independence from the empire)		The Church
Radicals (wanted overthrow of the regime, revolution)		

The Romanov family had ruled Russia for 300 years. Tsar Nicholas II was tsar in 1917. He seemed to be in a strong position with a large army, the support of the secret police (Okhrana) and power over the Duma (the Russian parliament). But all was to change.

The peasants

The peasants lived in poverty with rising population numbers making the poverty worse and famines a frequent threat.

- The peasants believed the answer to their poverty was more land. They wanted the land of the landowner class.

- In 1905, peasant unrest had swept through rural Russia, with peasants burning down landowner houses and taking landowner land. Brutal repression by the army had been used to end the unrest.

- In the First World War, over 15 million peasant men were called up to fight. The horses that peasants relied on for farm work were taken by the army. The army also **requisitioned** (took) peasant crops.

The town workers

Russia's industrialisation was concentrated in cities, often in huge factories employing thousands of workers.

- Living and working conditions in the cities were terrible: homes were overcrowded and working conditions were unsafe with long hours and harsh factory rules.

- When workers went on strike, factory owners would sack them or call the police or the army to break up the strike by force.

- In 1905, the industrial workers had joined with the middle-class liberals in a general strike that had nearly overthrown the tsar.

- In the First World War, economic problems meant many factories closed. Food prices also rose, making life very hard in the cities.

Organised opposition

Several different groups in Russia wanted change.

Radicals wanted to overthrow the tsarist regime and the ruling classes.	Liberals wanted more political freedoms to prevent revolution.	Conservatives wanted to defend the interests of the gentry.	Ultra nationalists wanted to protect the Russian Empire.

Socialist Revolutionaries (SRs) wanted a new society based on the peasant commune.

Social Democrats (SDs) were followers of **Karl Marx**. They were divided into:
- the **Bolsheviks** who believed they could lead the workers in revolution and help create communism on their behalf
- the **Mensheviks** who thought communism in Russia was a long way off because it was not yet industrialised.

Karl Marx was a German writer who died in 1883. He predicted the workers would lead a revolution to create a communist society where everyone was equal.

Now try this

Explain why liberal parties, which were keen to prevent revolution in Russia, were still a threat to the tsarist regime.

The First World War

The First World War plunged Russia into chaos. Military defeats undermined trust in the ruling classes, especially when Tsar Nicholas II took charge of the army and navy. Economic, social and political effects increased tensions in the countryside and in the cities.

Military defeats

Although Russia had the world's largest army in 1914, it was poorly led and badly equipped. The German generals were able to move their well-equipped and well-trained men around on an efficient railway network, then strike at the Russians where they were most vulnerable. By 1917, large areas of the western Russian empire had been lost to Germany.

Things were made worse by disrupted harvests, which reduced food supplies.

Economic effects of the war

The First World War was extremely expensive for all the major European powers. Russia faced additional economic pressures.

Germany blocked Russia's trade routes, factories were starved of raw materials and economic activity dropped. Taxes had to rise to help pay for the cost of the war.

⬇

To raise more money, the government arranged loans from its allies, increasing Russia's national debt.

⬇

The government printed more money to pay for the war. Inflation pushed up prices twice as fast as wages.

Political effects of the war

The **Duma** (Russian parliament) had supported the war at first but, as the crisis deepened, Duma deputies criticised the failures of the tsar's ministers.

⬇

In 1915, the Duma requested that the tsar replace his ministers with new ones supported by the Duma.

⬇

The tsar refused to share any power with the Duma. In response, the Duma became a centre of opposition to the tsar's government.

The tsar as commander-in-chief

- In August 1915, the tsar decided to take command of the Russian armed forces as commander-in-chief.
- His ministers warned him that this was a huge risk. The Russian people would blame the tsar directly for any further defeats.
- The tsar left Petrograd in September 1915 to move to army headquarters. He left his German wife, Tsarina Alexandra, as his **regent** – head of state in his absence.
- His actions lost him the respect of the military elite and the nobility – he had no military training and was away at war rather than in the capital.

Social effects of the war

- The conscription of 15 million peasant men and their horses to fight meant food production dropped. The army also requisitioned peasant crops and horses as well as prioritising the railway for the army. These factors meant there was less food for city populations as well as the countryside, leading to hunger and suffering.
- Possibly as many as 6 million refugees fled German occupation in the west. The government struggled to find them housing and food. Nationalist tensions increased.
- Economic problems meant many factory closures and job losses. Unemployment and food shortages meant growing social unrest.

Nicholas II visiting the Russian front during the First World War.

Now try this

In November 1916, a liberal leader in the Duma made a speech saying, 'We have many reasons for being discontented with this government, but these reasons all boil down to one general one: the incompetence and evil intentions of the present government.' Explain why this was seen as an attack on the tsar and tsarina as well as on the tsar's ministers.

Triggers for revolt

The February 1917 Revolution occurred because of a mixture of long-term discontent with the government and short-term triggers, such as food shortages and demoralisation of the army.

Strikes and demonstrations

Food shortages in Petrograd and Moscow increased social tensions; strikes in bakeries added to the food shortage crisis.

Timeline

18 February Strike at the Putilov Steelworks.

14 February Demonstration in support of the Duma.

23 February On International Women's Day, women joined striking workers in anti-government demonstrations; crowds grew ever larger when the government announced bread rationing might have to begin.

Late February Weather became unusually warm, encouraging people to join street protests.

23–25 February 250 000 people demonstrated in Petrograd – crowds became too big for police to control.

Mutiny in the army

Timeline

26 February evening Some soldiers were unhappy about what their officers were asking them to do. This mutiny was suppressed.

28 February A military report to the tsar declared that Petrograd was out of control.

26 February Soldiers were ordered to fire on demonstrators; 40 people were killed.

27 February Some regiments refused to obey orders to shoot.

Russia used the older Julian Calendar until February 1918, then switched to the Gregorian Calendar, the calendar most commonly used today. The dates in this guide follow the Julian Calendar until February 1918 and the Gregorian Calendar after that - other sources might give slightly different dates for events before February 1918.

The tsar's absence

On 22 February, Nicholas left Petrograd for army headquarters 780 km away, totally unaware of the rapidly growing crisis.

On 25 February, Nicholas sent an order to the police and army in Petrograd to end the unrest immediately.

Nicholas' decision to leave Petrograd and then to order the unrest to be suppressed led directly to his abdication.

The tsarina's rule

As regent, Tsarina Alexandra was unpopular with the people and with the Duma. She relied on the dubious advice of her friend, the mystical healer Rasputin, on how to govern, rather than the Duma. This infuriated the Duma who felt the tsarina should not be allowed to govern.

For more on the abdication, see page 4.

The tsar being away from Petrograd.

Food shortages in Petrograd.

Contempt for the tsarina.

Announcement of bread rationing.

The February Revolution: triggers for revolt

Mutiny in the army.

The International Women's Day March.

Unusually mild winter weather.

Demonstrations in support of the Duma.

Now try this There is information to help you on this page, but try to answer as many as you can from memory before checking.

Look at the spider diagram above. For each trigger: a) describe what happened, and b) explain how it contributed towards the February Revolution.

The abdication of the tsar

The February Revolution of 1917 succeeded in forcing the abdication of the tsar. After the abdication, Russia became a republic.

The Duma asked Nicholas to create a new cabinet involving Duma deputies.

This was Nicholas' last chance to save his throne by sharing some of his power but he was not capable of seeing how this could work.

↓

Nicholas refused and ordered the Duma to dissolve. Most government ministers left Petrograd.

The Russian Empire now had no real functioning government.

↓

Half the Duma (the liberals) refused to follow Nicholas' orders and carried on meeting.

This new Duma bloc was called the Duma Committee and went on to set up the Provisional Government.

↓

Army commanders suspected they could no longer rely on their troops to follow their orders.

Suppressing the revolution by force was too risky because of the fear of army mutiny throughout the Russian Empire.

The abdication

Army Command had two options:

1 Use soldiers from outside revolutionary Petrograd to crush the revolution.

2 Work with the Duma to find a political (non-violent) solution.

Option **1** did not seem possible because of the army mutiny: other troops might mutiny too.

Option **2** was put into action. Army leaders and Duma leaders met the tsar in Pskov. They suggested that the tsar must voluntarily give up the throne (abdicate) in order to save Russia.

↑

The leaders of the revolutionary parties were mostly living in exile at the time of the February Revolution. Lenin, leader of the Bolsheviks, was in Switzerland. In Petrograd, revolutionaries scrambled to try to take control of this unplanned revolution.

For more on Lenin, see page 8.

Nicholas hands over his written abdication statement in a railway carriage in the city of Pskov on his way back to Petrograd on 2 March. At first, Nicholas hoped his brother, Grand Duke Michael, would take over as tsar, but Michael refused and 300 years of Romanov rule in Russia was over. Russia had become a republic.

Now try this

On 27 February, Nicholas wrote in his diary, 'Disorders started several days ago in Petrograd; unfortunately even the troops have begun to take part in them. It is sickening to be so far away and to receive fragmentary bad news. I did not spend much time listening to reports. During the day I took a walk … the weather was sunny.' How useful is this quote in explaining Nicholas' abdication?

The Provisional Government

You need to know about the establishment of the Provisional Government and its relationship with the Petrograd Soviet, as well as about Kerensky's role as head of the Provisional Government.

The Provisional Government and the Petrograd Soviet

- At the same time as some Duma deputies were forming the Duma Committee, revolutionary groups were setting up the Petrograd **Soviet**.
- Across Petrograd, workers, soldiers and sailors elected representatives to the Soviet.
- When the tsar abdicated, 12 members of the Duma Committee formed the Provisional Government.
- The Provisional Government was set up with the approval of the Petrograd Soviet.
- The Petrograd Soviet's executive and the Provisional Government held meetings in the same place.

The Provisional Government

The Provisional Government was made up of politicians from a mix of parties, but most were either liberals or radical SRs. Its first acts included:

See page 1 for more about the parties involved.

- releasing political and religious prisoners
- promising full democratic freedom
- ending the death penalty
- taking over land belonging to the tsar
- transferring power to **zemstvos**.

The Provisional Government was also determined to continue with the war.

Key terms

Soviet – a committee of elected members (workers, soldiers and peasants).
Zemstvos – local councils.

The Petrograd Soviet

The Petrograd Soviet agreed to support the Provisional Government if **eight principles** were followed:

1. Amnesty for all political prisoners.
2. Freedom of speech, freedom of assembly, right to strike.
3. No privileges of class, religion or nationality.
4. Elections for a Constituent Assembly.
5. Elected people's militia to replace all police units.
6. Local government to be elected.
7. Military units that took part in the revolution to stay together, keep weapons and not be sent to the front.
8. Off-duty soldiers to have same rights as citizens.

The Petrograd Soviet had control over communications, over many ordinary soldiers and sailors, and over local efforts to improve food supplies. This caused problems for the Provisional Government.

Alexander Kerensky

Kerensky was a member of both the Provisional Government and the Petrograd Soviet and liaised between them. When he became leader of the Provisional Government in July 1917, he made some crucial mistakes:

- He continued to support the war, which angered ordinary soldiers.
- He acted against the old ruling classes, which lost him support from conservatives.
- He failed to control the Bolsheviks.

Alexander Kerensky, Russian officer and politician, 1917

Now try this

Look back at the reasons for discontent against the tsarist regime (page 1). Which was the main social group that benefited from the formation of the Provisional Government and why?

The main social groups in Russia were the peasants, the workers, the army, conservatives, liberals, radicals, the Church and members of ethnic minorities (non-Russians).

Weaknesses and failures

The Provisional Government and the network of soviets (headed by the Petrograd Soviet) were both trying to govern Russia: this is known as a time of Dual Power. It was an incredibly difficult time for any government, but Dual Power and the Provisional Government's own weaknesses led to the Provisional Government's collapse in October 1917.

Lack of decisive leadership.

Lack of control over the military – Order Number 1 meant the Petrograd Soviet had the final say on military matters, not the Provisional Government. Continuing to fight the war rather than only defending Russia's borders was very unpopular.

Continuing to fight the war – the June Offensive was a failure, making the Provisional Government's commitment to fighting the war even more problematic.

Weaknesses and failures of the Provisional Government

'Dual Power' meant the Provisional Government was in a very weak position and there were areas it had no control over, such as the railways and postal service.

Failure to improve the economy – no quick way to solve shortages.

More democracy and free speech meant more criticism of the government.

Failure to hold a general election.

Failure to provide more land for the peasants.

Lack of legitimacy – not elected by the people (unlike the soviets).

Kerensky and the June Offensive

Kerensky was War Minister when the Provisional Government decided to attack German and Austrian forces in June 1917. This became known as the June Offensive and was a disaster, with 200 000 Russian casualties and further losses of Russian territory. After the June Offensive, Kerensky took over the leadership of the Provisional Government from Prince Lvov.

A funeral for soldiers killed in the June Offensive, 29 June 1917.

Source A: From 'Order Number 1', published by the Petrograd garrison on 1 March 1917 and later by the Petrograd Soviet.

1. In all companies, battalions, regiments … and on the vessels of the navy, committees of elected representatives from the lower ranks of the above-mentioned military units shall be chosen …

2. The orders of the military commission of the State Duma shall be executed [carried out] only in such cases as they do not conflict with the orders and resolutions of the Soviet of Workers' and Soldiers' Deputies [the Petrograd Soviet].

Now try this

Study Source A, above. Explain why 'Order Number 1' undermined the authority of the Provisional Government.

The Kornilov Revolt

By August 1917, the Provisional Government was seriously weakened. Soldiers were angry with the government because of the June Offensive. Workers wanted the Petrograd Soviet to be in charge because they would benefit from that. Peasants wanted a government that gave them land. It was in this time of unrest that General Kornilov attempted to seize power.

Kerensky

> I have appointed Kornilov as commander of the army but I am not sure whether I support the army or the soviets. If Kornilov marches on Petrograd I can lead a defence against him and be the saviour of Petrograd.

General Kornilov

> I am worried about growing unrest in the towns and countryside. I am going to march on Petrograd to restore order.

The Kornilov Revolt

1. In July 1917, Kerensky made Kornilov head of the army in order to improve army discipline.

2. Kornilov and Kerensky agreed that more soldiers were needed in Petrograd.

3. However, Kornilov decided that Russia needed military rule. Kerensky saw this as a threat to the Provisional Government.

4. Kornilov sent troops to Petrograd on 24 August with orders to shut down the Petrograd Soviet.

5. Kerensky allowed the Bolsheviks to arm their supporters to defend Petrograd from Kornilov's troops. These armed supporters were named the Red Guards.

6. At the same time, railway workers blocked Kornilov's route to Petrograd and Bolsheviks met the troops and convinced them not to attack. The 'revolt' was over.

The Kornilov Revolt failed because his soldiers were no longer following orders and also because Petrograd workers acted to defend their revolution.

Significance of the Kornilov Revolt

✓ The Kornilov Revolt increased the popularity and influence of the Bolsheviks and weakened the Provisional Government further.

✓ Kerensky's plan to act as the saviour of Petrograd backfired. The people saw the Bolshevik Red Guards – not Kerensky – as having defended Petrograd and the revolution.

✓ The Bolsheviks had been predicting an attempt at counter-revolution, and the Kornilov Revolt seemed to prove them right.

✓ Any trust soldiers had for their officers was lost altogether. The establishment of the Red Guards to defend Petrograd gave the Bolsheviks a military advantage.

✓ On 31 August, the Bolsheviks won the most seats in the Petrograd Soviet election.

Now try this

Suggest **one** reason why Kornilov decided to order an attack on Petrograd.

Lenin's return

The Germans arranged for the Bolshevik leader, Lenin, to travel back through wartime Europe in a sealed train from his exile in Switzerland. They hoped that he would help knock Russia out of the war and give them one fewer enemy to fight. Lenin's return in April 1917 meant big changes for the Bolshevik Party.

This painting depicts Lenin's return to Petrograd in 1917 from his exile in Switzerland.

The 'April Theses'

In April 1917, Lenin set out a manifesto of how the working class should take control of Russia in a second revolution. His demands included:

1 End the war: a capitalist and imperialist conflict that threatened the revolution.

2 Transfer all power to the soviets: at every level of government, local to national. The Provisional Government should not be supported.

3 Take land from the rich landlords and give it to the peasants through agricultural soviets.

Growth of support for the Bolsheviks

The Bolsheviks were a small party in April 1917. Support for the Bolsheviks grew because:

- Lenin's April Theses meant the Bolsheviks had a clear and powerful message for workers, peasants and soldiers

- Bolshevik newspapers in most Russian cities constantly criticised the failures of the Provisional Government

- the Germans secretly sent money to the Bolsheviks to fund their campaigning.

Powerful messages

Lenin promoted simple but powerful new slogans for the Bolshevik Party.

ALL POWER TO THE SOVIETS!

Lenin said the power to govern Russia should all go to soviets – workers' soviets to run factories, agricultural soviets to run rural districts, regional soviets and city soviets, with congresses of soviets making decisions at national level.

The July Days

- Riots and demonstrations against the Provisional Government (3 July and 7 July 1917) turned into an uprising: the July Days.

- The uprising came about because of food shortages, and the failure of the June Offensive. The Bolsheviks did not start it.

- Lenin believed the time could be right to overthrow the Provisional Government. Bolsheviks joined the demonstrations.

- The Petrograd Soviet did not support the July Days. Its Menshevik members did not trust the Bolsheviks.

- The Soviet agreed to help the Provisional Government. Troops were moved into Petrograd and put down the uprising.

- Many Bolsheviks were arrested as they were blamed for starting the revolt. Lenin escaped, fleeing back to Finland in disguise.

PEACE, LAND AND BREAD

This slogan promised that if the Bolsheviks had control of Russia, they would end Russia's involvement in the war, give land to the peasants and end the food shortages in the cities.

Reactions to Lenin's return

Lenin's April Theses were a shock to the Bolshevik Party. Lenin had to work hard to persuade colleagues that Russia was ready for a second revolution. But his forceful personality and command of Marxist theory won the day.

Now try this

Explain what 'All power to the soviets!' meant.

The Bolsheviks seize power

In October 1917, Lenin decided this was the Bolsheviks' chance to seize power.

❶ Lenin's decision to seize power

The Kornilov Revolt in August 1917 increased Bolshevik support in Petrograd and humiliated the Provisional Government. By October 1917, the Bolsheviks had 340 000 members, 60 000 in Petrograd including 40 000 armed Red Guards. Despite the failure of the July Days, Lenin felt sure the time was right to overthrow the Provisional Government. On 10 October, Lenin secretly returned to Petrograd. In a long and stormy meeting with senior Bolsheviks, Lenin managed to convince his colleagues to support a new attempt to seize power.

❷ The Military Revolutionary Committee

- Rumours spread that the Bolsheviks were planning an armed takeover.
- Kerensky tried to send Bolshevik-influenced army units out of Petrograd.
- Trotsky, as leader of the Petrograd Soviet, convinced the Soviet to set up a Military Revolutionary Committee (the MRC) to bring together all the Soviet-supporting soldiers in Petrograd.
- By 21 October, most of Petrograd's regiments had promised loyalty to the MRC.

❸ Kerensky tries to stop the Bolsheviks

On 21 October, Kerensky ordered a crack down on the Bolsheviks:

- closing Bolshevik newspapers
- blocking river crossings between the city centre and working class districts
- calling for the arrest of the MRC.

Trotsky, as head of the Petrograd Soviet, used the MRC to take control of:

- road and canal bridges
- army headquarters
- telegraph offices.

Kerensky travelled around Petrograd in a car, looking for any soldiers who would defend the Provisional Government from the Bolsheviks.

❹ The Bolsheviks seize control

- On the night of 24–25 October, Red Guards seized more key areas of the city.
- There was almost no opposition. On the night of 25–26 October, Bolshevik soldiers climbed through the windows of the Winter Palace and arrested the remaining members of the Provisional Government.
- Many socialists left the Soviet in protest at the Bolsheviks' actions. On 26 October, Lenin formed a Bolshevik government called the Council of People's Commissars.

> The official Soviet view was that the October Revolution was a popular uprising led by Lenin. In fact, very few people in Petrograd were even aware that the Bolsheviks had seized power.

Lenin was single-minded with a clear plan of attack.

Lenin made sure the Bolsheviks were in charge and not any other revolutionary group.

Why was the October Revolution successful?

Kerensky didn't take the Bolshevik threat seriously after the July Days.

Kerensky didn't disband the Red Guards after the Kornilov affair.

The Provisional Government had become very unpopular and no one stood up to defend it.

Trotsky was an amazing planner who formed Red Guards into an effective fighting force.

Now try this

Answer this question using the arguments on this page and your own knowledge:

Was the unpopularity of the Provisional Government the most important reason for the October 1917 Revolution?

Remember that whatever conclusion you come to, you need to be able to explain how and why you have come to the conclusion. It may be helpful to draw a flowchart or spider diagram to organise your thoughts.

Early decrees and execution of the tsar

The Bolsheviks passed decrees at the Second All-Russian Congress of Soviets in November 1917 to live up to their promises. However, when the Bolsheviks lost the elections to the Constituent Assembly, they used force to hold on to power and to shut down any opposition.

1 **Decree on Peace (8 November 1917)**
- All countries should seek peace.
- Peace to be achieved without annexations (land seized) or indemnities (large fines).

2 **Decree on Land (8 November 1917)**
- Land taken from wealthy landowners now belonged to the peasants.
- In December, Church land was nationalised, too.

The early decrees

3 **Decrees on workers' rights (November–December 1917)**
- **Decree on Work** – 8-hour day.
- **Decree of Unemployment** – unemployment insurance for those unable to work.
- **Decree on Workers' Control** – workers' committees now ran their own factories.

4 **Decree on Nationalities (November 1917)**
- All different peoples of the old Russian Empire could have their own governments.
- However, these governments remained under Bolshevik control.

The abolition of the Constituent Assembly

- Lenin had promised to hold a general election for the Constituent Assembly: however, the SRs won with 53 per cent of the vote. The Bolsheviks got only 24 per cent.
- The Bolsheviks then declared that a return to parliamentary democracy was a backwards step when Russia already had soviets.
- The first meeting of the Constituent Assembly after the election was on 5 January 1918. It refused to pass the Bolsheviks' key decrees or to accept the principle of all power to the soviets.
- After one day, Lenin ordered the Red Guards to shut it down. It never reopened.
- Soon after, all political parties apart from the Bolsheviks were banned.

The Cheka

- On 7 December 1917, Lenin set up the Cheka – the Extraordinary Commission to Combat Counter-Revolution, Sabotage and Speculation.
- Lenin said that the revolution was under threat from the class enemies of the workers and peasants – the *burzhui* or bourgeoisie. The *burzhui* were people who had been middle class or upper class before the October Revolution.
- Bolshevik supporters often attacked anyone they suspected of being a *burzhui*. It was easy to denounce people to the Cheka as being *burzhui*: they would be arrested and their houses and property could then be taken by poor people.
- The Cheka became the main way in which the Bolsheviks used terror to consolidate their hold over Russia and the countries of the old empire.

The execution of the tsar and his family

- The former tsar, Nicholas, and his family were kept as prisoners by the Bolsheviks. In 1918 they were held in Yekaterinburg.
- Nicholas and the royal family were a potential threat to Bolshevik power. Monarchists could use them to rally support for a counter-revolution.
- On 17 July 1918, as anti-Bolshevik forces were closing in on Yekaterinburg, the Bolsheviks executed Nicholas, his wife and children, as well as four servants.

Tsar Nicholas II in March 1917: the tsar and his family were held captive in Yekaterinburg in the Ural mountains. Nicholas, Alexandra, their five children and four servants were all shot.

Now try this

Explain why Lenin abolished the Constituent Assembly.

The Treaty of Brest-Litovsk

One of the Bolsheviks' promises to the people was to take Russia out of the First World War. This was achieved with the Treaty of Brest-Litovsk on 3 March 1918.

The need for peace with Germany

1 Many Bolshevik supporters were soldiers and sailors who were desperate for an end to the war and a 'breathing space' as Lenin had promised.

2 Lenin said, 'We must make sure of throttling the bourgeoisie and for this we need both hands free.' Ending the war would mean the Bolsheviks could concentrate all their forces on wiping out political opponents within Russia.

3 Lenin and Trotsky were certain that there would soon be a revolution in Europe and any treaty they signed with Germany would no longer have any effect.

Significance of the treaty

In exchange for peace, Russia lost a huge area of its former western territories: Ukraine and the Baltic provinces, Finland and parts of Poland. It also lost Georgia (Stalin's homeland).
This meant the loss of:
- 74 per cent of Russia's coalmines and iron ore
- 50 per cent of its industry
- 26 per cent of its railways
- 27 per cent of its farmland
- 26 per cent of its population: 62 million people.

Russia also had to pay the Germans 300 million gold roubles.

Territories Russia lost in the Treaty of Brest-Litovsk.

The Treaty of Brest-Litovsk

- Lenin gave Trotsky the responsibility of negotiating a treaty with the Germans. None of the other allies came to the conference.

- Trotsky demanded a peace treaty with no losses to Russia. The Germans ended the ceasefire and advanced into Russia. It seemed possible that they would capture Petrograd.

- The Russians could do nothing to stop the German advance. Lenin demanded that Trotsky get a peace deal at any price.

- The treaty was signed on 3 March 1918.

There were different views about peace with Germany: the Left SRs wanted to continue the war; Lenin wanted to accept the German terms and peace; Trotsky wanted something in between. Lenin won.

Reactions to the treaty

👍 Soldiers were pleased that the war had ended, and Russians (and the Bolsheviks) were relieved that the threat of German invasion was over.

👍 The Bolsheviks believed that German workers would be disgusted by the harsh terms of the treaty. This would then be another reason for German workers to rise up in revolution, like the Russian workers.

👎 The Left SRs walked out of the government in protest at the treaty and they even assassinated the German ambassador, hoping to re-spark the war.

👎 Nationalists and conservatives were horrified at the losses to Russia and its empire. It became vitally important for many Russians to fight to stop the Bolsheviks, so that Russia could be saved from humiliation and destruction. They began to form into armies, the 'White armies', to fight the Bolsheviks, the 'Red Army'.

Revise the White and Red Armies on page 12.

The Treaty of Brest-Litovsk was a major cause of the Civil War.

Now try this

Explain how the Treaty of Brest-Litovsk was linked to the Bolsheviks' hopes for more revolutions in industrialised countries like Germany.

The Civil War

The Bolsheviks formed the Red Army and were opposed by the Whites, an alliance of anti-Bolshevik groups. The experience of civil war transformed the Bolsheviks' attitude to ruling Russia.

Reasons for the Civil War

- The huge territorial losses from the Treaty of Brest-Litovsk appalled many Russians.
- Nationalists and conservatives had everything to lose from the Bolsheviks' plans for a workers' and peasants' Russia.
- Former moderates, Mensheviks and some SRs opposed the Bolshevik dictatorship – they had wanted the Constituent Assembly.
- The Bolsheviks also made enemies of the 'Czech Legion', 40 000 Czech troops who took control of the Trans-Siberian Railway.
- Nationalities within the old Russian Empire wanted to break away from Russian control.
- Monarchists wanted to reinstate the tsar.

Effects of the Civil War on the Bolsheviks

- **Terror tactics to ensure control.** Once they had captured an enemy area, the Cheka, the Bolshevik political police, hunted down any suspected opponents and executed them.
- **Harsh discipline to ensure obedience.** Red Army deserters were shot. If a Red Army unit retreated, one man in every ten would be executed.
- **Ideological victory.** Winning the Civil War against so many opponents strengthened the Bolsheviks' belief in their revolution.
- **Centralised control.** The war strengthened the Bolsheviks' belief in highly organised control from the centre.
- **Russia under threat.** The involvement of former allies like France and Britain made the Bolsheviks fear foreign invasion.

Key events of the Civil War

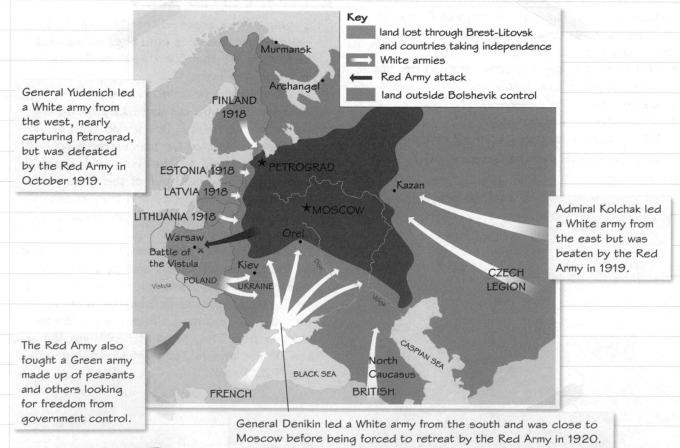

General Yudenich led a White army from the west, nearly capturing Petrograd, but was defeated by the Red Army in October 1919.

Key
- land lost through Brest-Litovsk and countries taking independence
- White armies
- Red Army attack
- land outside Bolshevik control

Admiral Kolchak led a White army from the east but was beaten by the Red Army in 1919.

The Red Army also fought a Green army made up of peasants and others looking for freedom from government control.

General Denikin led a White army from the south and was close to Moscow before being forced to retreat by the Red Army in 1920.

Now try this

Another reason for opposition to the Bolsheviks was that Lenin increasingly ignored the soviets and ruled through Sovnarkom, the Council of People's Commissars. Which groups within Russia would have been in opposition to the Bolsheviks because of this?

The Bolshevik victory

The reasons for the Bolshevik victory in the Civil War included the strength of the Bolsheviks, the role of Trotsky, lack of foreign intervention and the weaknesses of the Whites.

War Communism: introduced by Lenin to tackle the economic crisis.

The Red Army – conscription built the army up to a powerful fighting force of over 5 million soldiers.

Trotsky led the Red Army and reintroduced discipline, making it an effective and unified fighting force.

Control of central Russia – this meant shorter distances to supply their armies.

Bolshevik strengths in the Civil War

Effective propaganda: a constant message that only the Bolsheviks would look after ordinary Russians.

Central Russia also contained most of Russia's population – who could be conscripted into the Red Army.

Control of most of Russia's industries (for weapons) and railways.

Tactical alliances that meant not having to fight everyone at once.

For more on War Communism, see page 16.

The role of Trotsky in the Civil War

Trotsky, appointed Commissar for War in 1918, was more influential than Lenin in winning the Civil War.

- Trotsky organised the mobilisation of the Red Army into a huge fighting force.
- He realised the Red Army needed experienced ex-tsarist officers and kept their families hostage to ensure loyalty.
- Trotsky's **commissars** (political officers) kept strict discipline in the army and also spread Bolshevik propaganda.
- He encouraged soldiers to learn to read and write and taught them about the aims of the Bolsheviks.
- Trotsky introduced a Socialist Military Oath for all Red Army soldiers to swear. This was to encourage loyalty to the Bolsheviks.

Foreign intervention

- British, French, Japanese and US soldiers were all sent to help the Whites, and also to defend allied weapons dumps which had originally been sent to help Russia by its First World War allies.
- The foreign interventions helped the Whites for a while, and made them seem stronger than they really were.
- Bolsheviks used foreign intervention as propaganda: they urged that Russians should help the Reds prevent the foreign invasions.

US soldiers parading in Vladivostok, Russia, 1918.

Geographically very spread out – supplying White armies was difficult.

Foreign intervention to aid the Whites was a propaganda gift to the Reds.

Far fewer Whites than Reds: maximum 250 000 soildiers.

The Whites did not have large populations to conscript soldiers from; many troops would fight only for their own area.

White weakness in the Civil War

There was no single White leader: instead the leaders competed with each other.

The Whites did not control many industrial areas so supplying armies was more difficult.

Whites were not popular with workers and peasants.

The Whites did not share the same aims: monarchists, liberals and left wingers all disagreed about how they would run Russia.

Now try this

Explain why commissars were important in the Bolshevik victory in the Civil War.

The Red Terror and the Cheka

The Red Terror was a period of executions and arrests between September 1918 and February 1919. Lenin established this in order to get rid of anyone suspected of opposing the Bolsheviks. Ever since taking power, the Bolsheviks had steadily removed individual freedom in Russia. The Bolshevik state quickly became a dictatorship.

Timeline

The growth of the Bolshevik dictatorship

October 1917
Bolsheviks gained power.

November 1917
Revolutionary Tribunals introduced, replacing courts and lawyers.

December 1917
Liberal leaders arrested; non-Bolshevik newspapers banned. The Cheka established.

January 1918
Constituent Assembly shut down.

February 1918
'The Socialist Fatherland is in Danger' decree (allowed forced labour and execution for those who resisted).

June 1918
SRs and Mensheviks were arrested.

August 1918
Fanya Kaplan tried to assassinate Lenin: he survived being shot.

September 1918
Start of the Red Terror.

1921
All other political parties banned.

March 1921
The Kronstadt Mutiny

1922
Show trial of leading SRs – carried out as an example to others. SRs deported.

The role of the Cheka

The Cheka grew rapidly during the Civil War: by 1919 it had 100 000 employees.

The Cheka had enormous power: after 1918 the Cheka could arrest, imprison, torture or execute anyone they suspected. It is possible that as many as 12 000 people were executed by the Cheka between 1918 and 1920.

The Red Terror

- Lenin introduced the Terror after surviving an assassination attempt by an SR, Fanya Kaplan.
- The Bolsheviks called on all workers to report anyone who made any remarks against the soviets and their government. These 'class enemies' often went to prison camps.
- The Red Terror grew rapidly in the Civil War. As the Reds won back areas from White control, the Cheka was sent into the area to arrest anyone suspected of supporting the Whites or helping them in any way. Many were executed.
- The Terror was also used in the Red Army. The Cheka shot any deserters they recaptured.
- The Red Terror lasted from September 1918 to February 1919, but in fact its methods never went away under the Bolshevik dictatorship.

The Kronstadt Mutiny

- The Kronstadt naval base guarded Petrograd. Its sailors fought in the February Revolution, the July Days and the October Revolution.
- It was a shock to senior Bolsheviks, therefore, when the Kronstadt sailors rebelled against the Soviet government on 28 February 1921.
- Like many former Bolsheviks, the sailors were sick of War Communism, the way the Bolsheviks requisitioned food, the Red Terror and the lack of political freedom.
- Trotsky sent 50 000 Red Army soldiers to take back the base.
- There was fierce fighting and it took until 17 March for the sailors to be defeated: 500 were executed by the Cheka.
- The Kronstadt Mutiny did undermine the Bolsheviks' claim to be acting for the working classes and peasants. There were more protests against Bolshevik dictatorship and calls for 'soviets without Bolsheviks'.

For more on War Communism, see page 16.

Now try this

Explain how the Cheka helped the Bolsheviks keep hold of power in Russia.

Bolshevik centralisation

The Communist Party, as the Bolsheviks called themselves from 1918, believed that the state should control the economy, society and culture of the Soviet Union from the centre.

The Communist Party

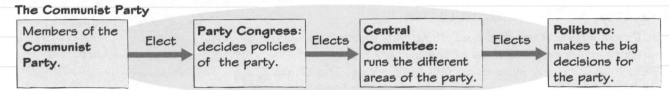

| Members of the Communist Party. | **Elect →** | Party Congress: decides policies of the party. | **Elects →** | Central Committee: runs the different areas of the party. | **Elects →** | Politburo: makes the big decisions for the party. |

Only Communist Party members can stand in elections

The Soviet government

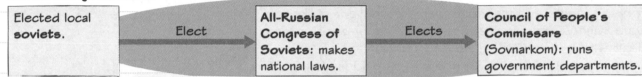

| Elected local soviets. | **Elect →** | All-Russian Congress of Soviets: makes national laws. | **Elects →** | Council of People's Commissars (Sovnarkom): runs government departments. |

The Soviet government and the Communist Party worked in parallel to rule the Soviet Union but in reality it was the Communist Party that determined what the Soviet government did.

All power to the soviets?

The All-Russian Congress of Soviets became a 'rubber stamp': it simply agreed whatever the government told it to. This made the Soviet Union a centralised dictatorship.

In 1919, the Communist Party elected a five-man Politburo; the five members were Lenin, Trotsky, Zinoviev, Kamenev and Stalin.

This became a central committee that decided party policy. Their decisions determined what happened in the Soviet Union. Ultimately, the soviets had no power at all.

The Communist Party was the only political party. There was no political choice. The only candidates at elections were Communist Party candidates.

Setting up of the USSR

In 1924, the lands of the old Russian Empire were reorganised into the Union of Soviet Socialist Republics (USSR).

The USSR was initially made up of the Russian Soviet Federated Socialist Republic (RSFSR), the Ukrainian Soviet Socialist Republic (SSR), the Belorussian SSR and the Transcaucasian SFSR.

The communist parties that ran the other republics all followed the orders of the All-Union Communist Party (of Bolsheviks) – the new name for the Communist Party from 1925 – led from Moscow. The parliament met infrequently, had very little power and all decisions were controlled by the party.

Now try this

Write a short paragraph to summarise Lenin's role in bringing about centralisation.

War Communism

War Communism was introduced in 1918. It put the Russian economy under government control. Lenin believed this was necessary if the Bolsheviks were to win the Civil War.

Features of War Communism

War Communism meant that everything in the economy was geared to meeting the needs of the military first.

- Peasants were not allowed to sell their crops. The Cheka requisitioned their crops for a fixed low price, and left the peasants a small amount for their own needs.
- Industries were nationalised and given production targets by the government.
- People's rights and freedoms were restricted: strikes were banned and any suspected political opposition was dealt with by the Cheka (the Red Terror).
- Money was abolished and people were paid in kind (paid in goods and services rather than in cash). Labour was also conscripted: the government forced people to work.

As a result, peasants tried to hide their grain. Peasants suspected of hoarding grain were shot.

Industrial production was targeted at meeting military needs. Production for consumers was not a priority.

Opposition continued and increased, for example, the Kronstadt Mutiny.

Transport problems meant industries did not get the raw materials they needed.

Workers started to leave the cities – either going into the Red Army or returning to villages to find food.

The collapse in industrial production meant there was nothing for the peasants to buy. Peasants stopped growing crops to sell to the cities.

The Bolsheviks needed control over industry to supply the Red Army with weapons and resources.

REASONS FOR WAR COMMUNISM

The Bolsheviks needed control over food supply in order to feed soldiers and workers.

After the October Revolution, banks stopped lending money to the government or industries.

The Treaty of Brest-Litovsk meant the loss of 40% of Russia's industries.

The Treaty of Brest-Litovsk meant the loss of major food production regions.

The Whites controlled some key agricultural regions.

Consequences of War Communism

- In 1920, farm production had fallen to 37 per cent of 1913 levels.
- The numbers of people working in factories fell by half, and production halved, too.
- Food shortages turned into famine. People were dying from starvation: in some areas people resorted to cannibalism.
- Industries were producing almost no consumer goods, increasing hardships in the cities.
- A black market developed: an illegal way of finding the consumer products and food that people needed, for high prices.
- In areas that the Reds did not control, and where money continued to be used, prices rose.

War Communism, an economic disaster and deeply unpopular, had to be abandoned.

Political crisis

- Factory workers organised protests and strikes over their falling living standards and lack of food. The Kronstadt Mutiny was linked to strikes in Petrograd: strikers had come to the naval base to ask for help.
- Communist Party members protested at the way they were excluded from decisions.
- There was a peasant uprising in Tambov Province.

War Communism was unpopular, but the Communist Party was able to blame a lot on the Whites and their occupation of farming and oil regions.

Now try this

The Bolsheviks promised peace, land and bread before the October Revolution. What happened to these promises under War Communism?

New Economic Policy (NEP)

War Communism may have helped win the Civil War, but protests against it threatened to overthrow the Communist Party's control of Russia and the other republics of the USSR. By 1921 the Soviet Union was in crisis. Lenin's response was the New Economic Policy (NEP).

This poster reads, 'From NEP Russia will come Socialist Russia'.

Reasons for NEP

The main reasons for the implementation of NEP in 1921 were:

1 the disastrous economic consequences of War Communism

2 the political opposition caused by War Communism.

Lenin recognised that the drive to socialism had been too fast and too rigorous.

Features of NEP

War Communism had introduced socialist features to the USSR. NEP reversed these:

- The free market was reintroduced. Now peasants could sell their produce and decide what price to sell it at.

- The state stopped requisitioning grain and other crops from the peasants: now peasants paid tax on what they sold.

- Money was reintroduced; workers were paid wages again.

- The state kept control of big factories, but small businesses and farms could be privately owned and run to make a profit.

- Foreign experts were brought in to improve how factories were run. These experts were paid more than ordinary workers.

Economic effects of NEP

1 Agricultural production increased as peasants began to produce more. Grain production in 1921 was 37 million tonnes. By 1923 it was 56 million tonnes (although it had been 80 million tonnes in 1913).

2 Industrial growth increased, but more slowly. The shortage of industrial products kept them expensive while food became cheaper. This was called the 'scissors crisis'. It meant peasants stopped producing so much food, leading to fears of more famine. The government cut prices for industrial products.

3 Some traders (NEP-men, NEP-women) made profits from the shortages of food and manufactured goods. Wealthier peasants also did well as they had the most surplus produce to sell. But this led to inequality within the USSR, which was not socialist.

Reactions to NEP

FOR	AGAINST
NEP was popular with peasants and traders. Although wealthier peasants did best from NEP, all peasants preferred the freedom to sell what they wanted rather than see the state requisition almost everything they produced.	Many Communist Party members did not like NEP as it was a backwards step that seemed to bring capitalism back to the USSR. It also gave the peasants what they wanted at the expense of the workers.

Now try this

Look at page 16 for information on War Communism.

Explain the key differences between War Communism and NEP.

Social changes

Social changes in the period 1918–24 included the impact of Bolshevik policies on women, on education and on culture.

Timeline

The impact of Bolshevik policies on women

1917
Women declared equal to men. 'Post-card divorces' made divorce easier. Non-religious marriage introduced.

1919
Zhenotdel, a women's organisation, was set up to increase freedom, equality and influence of women.

1920
Abortion made legal. Women's literacy increased with Civil War literacy campaigns.

The Bolsheviks wanted to liberate women from oppression by men. 'Post-card divorces' cost 3 roubles and the other partner was informed by post.

The leader of Zhenotdel was Alexandra Kollontai. Kollontai's influence was limited because she opposed Lenin by demanding more democracy in the Communist Party. Kollantai became the first woman ambassador; however, very few other women were promoted to top government positons.

In spite of these improvements in women's rights under NEP, the number of crèches declined, as did factory work for women, and women were still expected to do all the domestic work, even if they had a job as well.

Communist education policies, 1921–24

👍 Co-education (girls and boys taught together) was introduced, as a way of reducing discrimination against women.

👍 There was a major literacy drive in the Red Army.

👍 Peasants were encouraged to learn to read and write.

👍 By 1926, about 58 per cent of the population was literate, a big increase from before the revolution.

Although literacy rates did increase, it was difficult for the Communist Party to make as much progress as it wanted, because economic problems limited investment.

This poster from 1920 says, 'In order to have more it is necessary to produce more. In order to produce more, it is necessary to know more.'

Communist cultural policies

The Communist Party understood the power of propaganda in convincing people to support their revolution. Agitprop was the Agitation and Propaganda Section of the Central Committee Secretariat of the Communist Party: the party's propaganda wing. It used art, literature, film and music to promote communist ideas and portray the USSR's communist future.

Controlling communist art

The 1920s were a time of great artistic freedom as artists with new ideas (known as *avant-garde*) experimented with different ways to represent communism. However, the Communist Party needed artists to help spread propaganda. Artists were increasingly censored by the state department Glavlit, which ensured that books, pictures, film, music, dance and other art forms all showed communism in an accessible and very positive way, called 'socialist realism'.

Now try this

Why was the Communist Party interested in making workers and peasants literate?

Stalin leads the USSR

After Lenin's death in 1924, there was a struggle for power among the senior communists to become leader of the Soviet Union. Just before he died, Lenin had written a 'testament' criticising all the other senior communists, but each of the main rivals had different strengths and weaknesses.

Stalin

Ideology: Believed in 'Socialism in One Country': that the USSR could become a socialist state on its own.

👍 Position as General Secretary: power to appoint supporters to key party jobs.

👍 Appearance of moderation: no extreme views, always respectful to rivals. Kept private opinions to himself.

👎 Lenin's testament criticised his rudeness and lust for power.

👎 Seen as boring, unlike many key rivals.

Trotsky

Ideology: Believed in 'Permanent Revolution': that communism needed revolutions to spread from country to country. Believed in rapid industrialisation rather than NEP.

👍 Brilliant speaker.

👍 Lenin's close comrade through the revolution and Civil War.

👍 His organisation and leadership key to Red victory in Civil War.

👎 Arrogant and bossy.

👎 Menshevik until 1917, unlike the others, who were longstanding Bolsheviks.

👎 Lack of supporters outside the military.

Zinoviev and Kamenev

👍 Worked closely together, strengthened them both.

👍 Zinoviev was party boss in Petrograd, Kamenev in Moscow.

👍 Worked closely with Stalin to run the party and weaken Trotsky after Lenin's death.

👎 The only two senior Bolsheviks to oppose Lenin's plan to seize power in October 1917.

👎 Power was limited to Petrograd and Moscow, while Stalin controlled the party.

Bukharin

👍 Very popular within the party.

👍 Excellent writer and theorist: editor of *Pravda* (party newspaper).

👎 Argued strongly against Treaty of Brest-Litovsk, which was later used against him.

👎 The main supporter of NEP, which many Bolsheviks viewed as capitalist.

Key steps to Stalin as leader

Stalin made sure that he took the lead role at Lenin's funeral, which Trotsky was too ill to attend.

⬇

Stalin then worked with Kamenev and Zinoviev (with Bukharin's support) to undermine Trotsky. But when Kamenev and Zinoviev then opposed Bukharin, Stalin criticised them for trying to split the party.

⬇

Economic difficulties in 1927–28 put pressure on NEP, which Bukharin supported. Stalin switched to arguing for rapid industrialisation and the collectivisation of agriculture. Stalin won the party's support and Bukharin lost his influence.

Now try this

Explain how Stalin used his position as General Secretary of the Communist Party to get rid of his rivals for power.

The purges

The purges were a continuation of Bolshevik use of violence to eliminate opposition, but under Stalin there was a change in the scale of purges: both the reasons for them and their consequences.

Timeline

The purges

1933
18% of party members expelled as unsuitable or disloyal.

1936
First show trials: 16 senior party members. including Zinoviev and Kamenev.

1938
Last great show trial; Bukharin shot. Purge spreads to NKVD.

1931
Ex-Mensheviks shot as 'wreckers'.

1934
Kirov murdered.

1937
Show trial of 17 more senior party members: all were found guilty. NKVD (secret police) begin mass arrests. Purge of the military.

1941
The purges had sent around 8 million people to labour camps.

Kirov's assassination

Stalin's policies in farming and industry caused big problems in the Soviet Union. By the 1930s, the party started to criticise Stalin. Even Kirov, one of his closest allies, called for a policy change. Stalin suspected Kirov wanted to take the leadership from him. Kirov was assassinated in December 1934. Stalin claimed that a huge conspiracy, led by Trotsky, was responsible. After Kirov's death, Stalin purged the party of potential rivals. These purges spread to the whole of Soviet society.

Economic problems
Accidents and economic under-performance blamed on imaginary 'wreckers'.

Stalin's fear of Kirov
Kirov became very popular. Did Stalin order Kirov's assassination, and then use it to remove rivals?

Reasons for the purges

Stalin's paranoia
Stalin had made it to the top, but then became paranoid about any possible rivals to power.

Following Lenin's example
The Red Terror during the Civil War was a precedent for the purges.

Attack on the party and government
After the purges linked to Kirov, arrests focused on party members and government staff accused of not following orders.

Mass terror (Yezhov)
The NKVD had targets for the arrests. They forced those arrested to name others. Under Yezhov's leadership of the NKVD (1937–38), no one was safe.

Nature of the purges

Forced confessions
Those arrested were beaten until they confessed to any crime they had been accused of. But many never knew why they had been arrested.

Use of Gulags
The Gulag was the state system of labour camps. By 1941 there were 8 million in the camps, with perhaps a further million in prisons.

Consequences of the purges

1 **Stalin dominant:** Stalin's purges terrified everyone else into obedience. No one dared to question his leadership.

2 **'Old Leninists' destroyed:** the Bolsheviks who had built the Communist Party with Lenin were dead. No one now could challenge Stalin. New party members all owed their position to Stalin.

3 **Chaos in government and the economy:** the loss of so many experienced managers, administrators and specialists left the government and industry with a serious shortage of skills.

4 **Weakened armed forces:** there was no evidence of any military plot against Stalin, but the purge of the military killed off most of Stalin's experienced officers. Soldiers arrested by the NKVD often accused their officers in turn. This loss of military leadership and experience seriously weakened the armed forces and was to prove a significant setback when Germany invaded Russia in 1941.

Now try this

Write a paragraph explaining the key effects of the purges on Soviet society.

The NKVD, Gulag and show trials

Stalin's terror was administered by the secret police, NKVD, who received the quotas for the numbers of enemies of the people to be arrested, made the arrests required and then processed millions of their fellow citizens through interrogation, trial, sentencing, execution or incarceration.

Stalin's terror

Stalin used existing Bolshevik systems for his purges:

- **Secret police** – Stalin used the OGPU, a new version of the Cheka (later known as the NKVD and then the KGB).

- **Gulags** – these labour camps were a new version of the Bolsheviks' prison camps. The secret police used terror to get confessions. People were arrested in the middle of the night, tortured and deprived of sleep, and their families and friends were threatened, until they signed confessions to made-up crimes.

- **Terror** – Stalin's terror was similar to the climate of fear in the Civil War.

These systems were descendants of tsarist secret police and labour camps, too.

The work of the NKVD

NKVD roles included: intimidation (scaring people into conforming to the system), arresting people, forcing confessions through repeated interrogation (the 'conveyor system'); running prisons; and executing people. From 1935, three-man teams of NKVD officers decided whether people were innocent of the charges against them, or guilty. There was no other legal process, for example, no defence.

After the initial purges linked to Kirov's murder in 1934, the head of the NKVD was executed for not having acted faster to track down enemies. After that, the NKVD were given quotas of 'enemies of the people' to find. Mass arrests of innocent people followed.

Conditions in the Gulags

In the Gulags: prisoners were used as slave labourers ('white coal') to extract resources and build infrastructure for the Soviet Union.

The people sent to Gulags were from all parts of Soviet society.

For more on kulaks, see page 24.

Gulag inmates working on a large-scale infrastructure project: these men had been sent to the Gulag during collectivisation, accused of being **kulaks** (rich peasants).

Inmates had only thin uniforms, miserable food and shacks to live in. They endured long hours of hard physical labour. The death toll was very high: perhaps 2 million people.

Camps were spread right across the USSR, including many in northern and eastern parts of the Soviet Union, where winters were severe.

The show trials, 1936–38

Only high-profile leading party members (like Zinoviev and Kamenev) had show trials. The public declarations of guilt were meant to make the Soviet people believe the country really was under attack by enemies of the people. These enemies could then be blamed for all the Soviet Union's problems.

Show trials were important because they justified all the mass arrests. Ordinary people were convinced that enemies were everywhere. They also gave ordinary workers the power to denounce their managers and people they did not like to the NKVD.

Now try this

'The monstrousness of my crimes is immeasurable especially in the new stage of the struggle of the USSR. May this trial be the last severe lesson, and may the great might of the USSR become clear to all.' This statement was made by Bukharin at his show trial in 1938. How does this statement help explain why Stalin ordered show trials of famous 'Old Bolsheviks' like Bukharin?

Official culture and the new Constitution

Censorship is when the state controls what people see, hear and read. In the USSR the state controlled all media, even art and music. Propaganda is information given out to spread ideas or points of view. In the USSR all state information was propaganda, including the new Constitution of 1936.

Media: Propaganda films were shown all over the USSR, giving a false picture of how well everything was going.

Media: Artists, writers, film-makers, singers and so on were all employed by the state and commissioned to create things glorifying the Soviet Union.

Media: Records from the past were changed; for example, photos featuring Trotsky and Lenin were altered to show only Lenin.

Media: Everything that was read or listened to had to be positive about the USSR. Books by 'enemies of the people' like Trotsky were suppressed. Glavlit turned economic data into propaganda, too: only good economic results were published.

Media: Socialist realism was a type of art that always showed Soviet life in the most optimistic way. It was designed to help ordinary people understand what socialism was supposed to be achieving: a better life for everyone.

Soviet propaganda and censorship

Education: New curriculums were drawn up that praised Stalin's achievements. School textbooks had to be approved by the state and set out Stalin's view of each subject.

Education: A new generation of Communist teachers brought back discipline to schools. Previously, radical students had denounced unpopular teachers to the NKVD.

Religion: Communists were atheists and all religions came under pressure; places of worship were shut, religious education was banned. There were attacks on Muslims in southern SSRs.

The new Constitution of 1936

👍 It replaced the Congress of Soviets with the Supreme Soviet of the USSR.

👍 Instead of only some people being allowed to vote, everyone was allowed.

👍 Instead of voting being open, it was done in secret so no one could see how you voted.

👍 It guaranteed workers' rights to holidays, health care, housing, education and other benefits.

👍 It gave the 15 republics of the USSR the same rights as Russia.

👎 People could all vote but there was only one party to vote for.

👎 Workers had lots of rights but these rights could all be ignored by the secret police.

👎 The activities of all the republics of the USSR were closely controlled from Moscow by the Communist Party.

👎 Stalin ignored the Constitution and ran the USSR as a dictatorship.

The new Constitution was mostly propaganda, persuading ordinary people to support the Soviet Union. Stalin also wanted to give a good impression to other countries, particularly Germany. However, in reality the brutality of life in the USSR continued.

Now try this

Suggest **three** consequences for Soviet society of such extensive state censorship and propaganda.

The cult of Stalin

After Lenin's death, a cult of Lenin began in which Lenin became an infallible leader – someone who was never wrong. The cult of Stalin continued this theme: Stalin became 'the Lenin of today'.

Stalin as the 'Lenin of today'
Stalin portrayed himself as the person best able to understand Lenin's ideas and put them into practice.

Focus on Stalin's economic 'achievements'
Stalin was shown on posters surrounded by modern factories, successful collective farms and happy, prosperous people.

The cult of Stalin

'Leader, Teacher, Friend'
Stalin was given a very friendly image and was often shown surrounded by happy children. He was shown as the father of the whole country.

Reasons for the cult of Stalin

- Setting up Stalin as the perfect leader, like Lenin, gave the Soviet people confidence that all the hardships and sacrifices were worth it: they were building socialism together.

- The long-standing tradition in Russia of the ruler being a father for the whole country fitted well with Stalin's portrayal as 'Leader, Teacher, Friend'.

- The cult was needed in order to gain support for the regime: although local party members might make a mess of everything, Stalin would be able to put everything right.

A poster cultivating the image of Stalin as a fatherly figure.

How the cult of Stalin was achieved

The cult of Stalin was encouraged (cultivated) through art, propaganda, literature and rewritings of history.

- **Art**: Stalin's image as 'Leader, Teacher, Friend' was depicted in paintings, murals and statues all over the USSR. Artists reimagined him as Lenin's closest friend (which he was not) and as the mastermind of the October Revolution or the Reds' Civil War victory (instead of Trotsky).

- **Propaganda messages**: Stalin was always careful to say that Lenin, the USSR and its people were more important than he was.

But Stalin's face was everywhere, and his policies and reforms were constantly praised as though he was superhuman.

- **Books, poems and plays**: authors, playwrights and poets praised Stalin for his achievements. Soviet history books gave Stalin a leading role in the key events of the Bolsheviks' rise to power; for example, the October Revolution and the Civil War.

 The cult of Stalin was very popular in the Soviet Union. People genuinely believed that Stalin wanted to help them, and would write to him for advice and help. Sometimes he would reply, which was then widely reported.

Source A: From *Joseph Stalin*, a collection of articles about Stalin by Helen Rappaport, published in 1999.

Stalin was seen as having superhuman powers – 'taller than the Himalayas, wider than the ocean, brighter than the sun' (in the words of a poet). Stalin became the modern 'little father' to the great mass of Russian peasants – a term traditionally applied to the Tsars.

Now try this

What **two** things can you infer from Source A about the cult of Stalin?

23

Collectivisation

Collectivisation ran from 1928 to 1933 and was Stalin's solution to the economic and ideological problems of peasant agriculture in the Soviet Union, and to his political problems with Bukharin.

Falling grain production
Grain production started to fall under NEP. In 1927 grain collection fell below levels needed to feed the cities.

Communist ideology
Marx taught that communism was built by proletarian workers: peasant farming should have disappeared.

Concerns about NEP
NEP favoured individual peasant farmers selling grain for profit – this looked like capitalism.

Reasons for collectivisation

Stalling industrial production
Without cheap grain to feed workers, Soviet industry was plateauing under NEP.

Stalin's rival, Bukharin
Bukharin supported NEP, so Stalin could attack him by attacking NEP.

Problems of NEP

Many of the reasons for Communist Party support for the collectivisation reforms were reactions against the impacts of NEP in the countryside and on industrial development.

👎 Many in the party hated the idea that kulaks were benefiting most from NEP, while workers were having to pay more for their food.

👎 Socialism and communism were about collective efforts for the good of everyone. But NEP was encouraging the opposite: private peasant farms run for profit.

👎 Peasant agriculture was not modernising, so yields were still low. Instead of using tractors, peasants still ploughed with horses and farmed using centuries-old traditions.

👎 In 1927–28 there was a grain procurement crisis: not enough grain was collected to feed the urban populations of the Soviet Union.

The organisation of collectives

Collective agriculture was completely different from peasant agriculture.

- The state owned the land, the equipment and everything the land produced.

- The state told each collective farm (kolkhoz) what to farm and set it a production target. The state paid a set (low) price when it took this.

- All collective farm workers were organised into brigades and worked set hours.

- Collective farms were mechanised – tractors and combine harvesters were allocated from Machine Tractor Stations (MTS). Secret police kept an eye on each collective farm from the MTS.

- Each collective farm was also set a quota of produce that it was allowed to keep in order to feed its workers.

Attack on kulaks

1927–28	**1929**	**1930**	**1931–32**
Grain was taken by force from peasants because of the grain crisis. Peasants were forced to join kolkhozes with Red Army pressure. Many refused and were labelled 'kulaks'.	Stalin launched a campaign of dekulakisation: 'liquidation of the kulaks'. Peasants were shot or exiled to Siberia.	30 000 kulaks died between 1930 and 1931. Peasants continued to resist collectivisation. Stalin halted the scheme and peasants returned to their farms.	Stalin revitalised the collectivisation campaign. Famine struck USSR.

Now try this

What role did the Red Army play in making sure Stalin's policy of collectivisation was implemented?

Collectivisation: successes and failures

Collectivisation did have successes, including increased grain supply to boost industrialisation and to export to the rest of the world. But the human cost of collectivisation was huge.

Successes of collectivisation

👍 By 1933, 83 per cent of all arable land and 64 per cent of all peasant households had been collectivised. By 1935, 90 per cent of farmland had been collectivised.

👍 Prior to the MTS there had been very little mechanisation in farming, so the MTS did bring improvements.

👍 Many more young people from rural areas went to agricultural school and learned about modern farming methods.

👍 Rationing of bread, and many other foods, was ended by 1934; by 1935, the steep fall in grain production had begun to recover.

👍 The USSR increased its grain exports to other countries, which earned the USSR money to invest in industrialisation.

👍 Huge numbers of peasants left the land and moved to the cities. These people provided the workforce for the USSR's rapid industrialisation.

👍 Getting control over the countryside was a political success for Stalin: many in the Communist Party had disliked the power NEP gave the peasantry.

Collectivisation was an efficient way for the state to take as much as it needed from agriculture in order to industrialise the USSR: the state controlled food supply.

Failures of collectivisation

👎 The famine of 1932–33: peasants who had destroyed their crops and livestock had nothing to eat. Stalin probably refused to help because of peasants' opposition to collectivisation. At least 3.3 million people died.

👎 The 'liquidation of the kulaks' policy killed or removed many of the most experienced farmers from Soviet agriculture.

👎 Stalin allowed kolkhoz peasants to keep their own small private plots: about 30 per cent of the USSR's food products came from the private plots, although they made up only 1 per cent of the farming area.

👎 There were too few tractors and most were poorly made and constantly needed to be repaired.

👎 Because so many peasants fled to the cities, internal passports were introduced: this made it very difficult to leave the collective farms.

👎 Kolkhozniks (collective farm workers) did as little work as they could get away with. Soviet agriculture was still very inefficient, with low productivity.

After collectivisation, there was a fall in living standards in both the city and the countryside compared with standards under NEP.

Famine in Ukraine, 1932–33

- The Red Army had defeated Ukrainian nationalists in the Civil War.
- Many Ukrainian peasants refused to join collective farms because they saw it as a new form of serfdom.
- To help crush the resistance to collectivisation, the state took more and more grain away from Ukraine, even as the people there were starving.
- All the time, the Soviet government denied there was any famine and refused foreign aid. Around 3 million Ukrainians are thought to have died in this deliberate famine.

Bread and grain being confiscated from a Ukrainian village during the famine of 1932–33.

Now try this

'The failures of collectivisation were far greater than its successes.' To what extent do you agree with this statement?

Industrialisation

Stalin and the Communist Party wanted an industrialised USSR for ideological reasons, and to defend the Soviet Union against its enemies. Industrialisation was organised by the state, through Five-Year Plans.

Ideological motives
Marxism taught that socialist countries would be industrialised countries, with industry under the control of the workers – the USSR needed to follow this.

Industrial stagnation under NEP
The 'scissors crisis': as food prices dropped, peasants had less money to buy manufactured goods. Industrial production could not grow without a market.

Motives for rapid industralisation

Stalin's political motives
Stalin's rival Bukharin supported NEP and was against rapid industrialisation. As problems increased under NEP, Stalin argued for rapid industrialisation and undermined Bukharin.

The Five-Year Plans

In 1926, the Communist Party agreed that rapid industrialisation should happen on an enormous scale. Gosplan, the State Planning Committee, had the job of planning industries across the USSR.

1 The First Five-Year Plan (1928–32) focused on increasing output of heavy industry, e.g. steel-making, engineering, chemicals.

2 The Second Five-Year Plan (1933–37) also focused on increased output of heavy industry, but with greater efficiency. There was also to be increased output of some consumer products.

3 The Third Five-Year Plan (1938–41) focused on an increase in military production, and improvements to education.

Gosplan

- Gosplan was responsible for setting targets for all the key industries to meet.

- This involved setting up new factories as well as organising existing ones: 5000 new factories were set up from 1928 to 1937.

- Enormous pressure was put on managers and workers to deliver the targets, putting emphasis on quantity rather than quality.

- If workers and managers met their targets, they could be rewarded with higher wages.

Planning the industrial production of a whole country was very complicated. The targets set for different industries were often far more than they could achieve. Industries therefore sometimes reported false production figures back to Gosplan. This made Gosplan's targets even less realistic!

The Stakhanovite Movement

- Aleksey Stakhanov was a coalminer who became famous for mining 14 times his quota.

- Soviet propaganda made him a celebrity and encouraged all workers to become **Stakhanovites** and to try to over-fulfil their targets to help meet the plan early.

- Stakhanov's mining feat was more propaganda myth than reality: he had a lot of help and high-quality equipment.

The Stakhanovite movement had mixed effects. Managers who had blocked Stakhanovite demands were often purged in Stalin's terror.

For more on terror under Stalin, see pages 20 and 21.

Aleksey Stakhanov explaining his system to a fellow worker. One problem with the Stakhanovites was that they disrupted factory routines and made managers' jobs more difficult. Also, non-Stakhanovites found it harder to find places to live and to get decent wages.

Now try this

Write **one** paragraph outlining the key features of industrialisation under Stalin.

Industrialisation: successes and failures

Industrialisation through the Five-Year Plans created a massive growth in industry in the Soviet Union, but its products and processes were low quality and inefficient, and ignored the consumer.

Increases in production

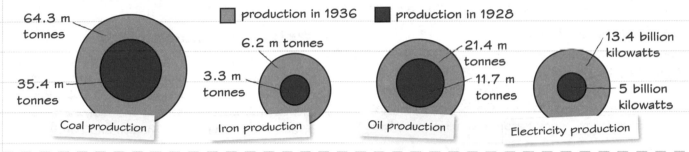

■ production in 1936   ■ production in 1928

64.3 m tonnes
35.4 m tonnes
Coal production

6.2 m tonnes
3.3 m tonnes
Iron production

21.4 m tonnes
11.7 m tonnes
Oil production

13.4 billion kilowatts
5 billion kilowatts
Electricity production

Failures of industrialisation

👎 Some production depended on slave labour from the Gulags.

👎 Factory conditions were often dangerous.

👎 Living conditions for some did not improve with many living in tents and having to queue for basic items because of a shortage of consumer goods.

👎 Targets meant quality was compromised and many goods broke easily.

👎 Productivity was low compared with other industrialised countries.

👎 There was waste and confusion because of inefficient production techniques and lack of communication and supporting transport.

👎 Targets were set low or missed targets were overlooked – factory managers could not be trusted to give accurate figures.

Interpreting industrialisation

Stalin's industrialisation of the USSR was very impressive because it transformed a peasant country into a modern, industrialised country. Stalin told his followers, 'We are becoming a country of metal, cars and tractors.' The USSR became an increasingly urbanised country, as people moved from the countryside to live and work in the cities. This progress was organised and directed by the state.

However, rapid industrialisation caused chaos in the Soviet economy. Raw materials often never arrived and there were often no spare parts to repair broken machinery. The only way to meet targets was to lie about production, or to make such low-quality products that they broke as soon as they were used. Managers faced constantly changing production targets.

Successes of industrialisation

👍 The USSR was now a fully industrialised nation.

👍 Increase in production of arms helped eventually to repel the German invasion during the Second World War.

👍 Supply of raw materials increased.

👍 New towns and cities, such as Magnitogorsk, were built.

👍 There was no unemployment.

👍 Huge new factories and industrial complexes were built.

👍 The Communist Party had more support from industrial workers than from rural peasants.

A propaganda poster from the early 1930s shows Soviet industrial production increasing rapidly and in a modern way, while in the capitalist countries of France, England, Germany and USA, industrial production is going downhill, as the system that supports these countries collapses.

Now try this

To what extent do you think that Stalin's industrialisation of the USSR was a success?

Living and working conditions

By 1941, living conditions in the Soviet Union had changed greatly for most people. Under the tsarist regime, the majority of people had been very poor. After the economic and social changes of 1928–39, living conditions were generally better; however, socialism was supposed to remove the class divisions that made workers poor and factory owners rich, but in fact the workers were still a lot worse off than the party bureaucrats.

Living conditions

Housing conditions were basic but better than they had been before 1928. Space was the main problem, with families restricted to living in one or two rooms. Conditions on the collective farms were harsher than in the cities.

Working conditions

Workers were given holidays, days off, housing, health care and free education but trade unions were banned and workers were often not allowed to change jobs. Conditions in the factories were poor and there was limited health and safety.

Life in towns

- **Housing**: some workers still lived in barracks; many families shared communal housing.
- **Food**: food was rationed until 1935, with four grades of ration. The lowest grade of ration did not include any meat or fish. Industrial workers received the high ration grade.
- **Working conditions**: there was little concern about worker safety and harsh laws punished lateness to work and unauthorised time off. Pay and conditions were, however, better than for rural workers.
- **Personal freedom**: internal passports (1932) restricted people's ability to move. Secret police kept close control over everyone's lives.

Life in the countryside

- **Housing**: there was little investment in collective farms and housing remained basic.
- **Food**: collective farm workers had very low pay and did not own the crops they grew for the state. Most depended on their very small garden plots to grow food to eat.
- **Working conditions**: working life was very hard with very few rewards. The farm workers resisted the conditions imposed on them by working as slowly as they dared.
- **Personal freedom**: collective farm workers were the lowest social group in the USSR. Internal passports aimed to keep them in their place. Despite the risk of being arrested and sent to the Gulag, thousands tried to escape the countryside.

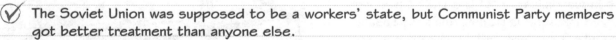

In both rural and urban workplaces, men tended to earn more than women.

Privilege and the party

- ☑ The Soviet Union was supposed to be a workers' state, but Communist Party members got better treatment than anyone else.
- ☑ Party members had better housing, better jobs and special perks like holidays and access to leisure clubs.
- ☑ However, under Stalin's rule no one was free as everyone lived in fear of being reported or arrested.

Now try this

Study this propaganda poster. How does it portray life in the Soviet Union? Do you think it is an accurate picture of what Soviet life was like?

The words on this poster read 'Day after day, life becomes even happier'.

: КАЖДЫМ ДНЕМ ВСЕ РАДОСТНЕЕ ЖИТ

Changes for women and the family

In 1928 there were 3 million women working; by 1940, there were 13 million women working. However, men still held all the important jobs and in 1936 divorce and abortion were made much more difficult to obtain.

Women and the Bolshevik reforms

After the revolution, the Bolshevik government introduced several reforms affecting women:

- divorce was made simple
- abortion and contraception were easy to obtain
- women had equal pay for equal work
- there were equal educational opportunities.

These reforms had been designed to break up the bourgeois traditions of marriage, and to free women to be the equals of men in every area.

Changes for women under Stalinism

By the 1930s, Stalin had decided that marriage and the family should now be reinforced:

1 Birth rates were falling, while Stalin wanted a growing population for industrialisation.

2 Stalin did not like some of the social impacts that came with easy divorces. There were gangs of unruly children on the streets, which was blamed on divorces and absent fathers.

3 The party was dominated by men who still believed that women were not their equals.

Abolition of Zhenotdel (1930):
Zhenotdel was the women's section of the Communist Party.

Controls on contraception and abortion:
Abortions were banned in 1936. Sterilisations were banned and the state made it difficult to obtain contraceptives.

Changes in the position of women after 1936

Stricter conditions for divorces (1936):
Higher fees were charged for divorces (50 roubles for the first divorce, 150 for the second). Child support payments were raised (starting at 25 per cent of wages for one child).

Incentives for women to have children:
Mothers who had six children or more received 2000 roubles a year for five years – a very large amount of money.

Changes in women's employment

Female train workers, 1935: this was one squad of a limited number of all-female train crews.

Women made up 40 per cent of all industrial workers in 1937, a far greater percentage than in 1928, but there were very few women in managerial positions and women tended to earn less than men. Also, most jobs were in industries that traditionally employed women, such as textiles.

Changes in the political position of women

In 1930, the women's section of the Communist Party, Zhenotdel, was closed. It had been Zhenotdel that convinced the Bolshevik Party to legalise abortion in 1920.

Zhenotdel was successful at organising groups focused on issues concerning women, but party leaders grew concerned that these groups were a challenge to mainstream (male-dominated) communism.

When Zhenotdel was shut down in 1930, the official reason was that all women's issues had been solved under socialism. In fact, women's rights were under increasing attack.

Now try this

Officially, the Soviet Union had equality between men and women. Suggest **two** ways in which women's lives were, in fact, very far from being equal with men's in the Soviet Union.

Persecution of ethnic minorities

The Soviet Union was made up of 15 republics and hundreds of different ethnic groups. Russians were the ethnic majority (55 per cent): Soviet policy towards ethnic minorities changed over time.

Socialist theory on nationalism

Socialist theory said that proletarians were the same everywhere and that being a worker was far more important than being a Russian, or a Georgian, or a Finn. Socialism was internationalist, not nationalist.

The Bolsheviks and nationalism

The Soviet Union (created 1922) was a collection of hundreds of different ethnicities. Some of these had very strong national identities, like Ukrainians. The Bolsheviks decided to encourage people to be proud of their different languages and traditions, but this was to be organised through soviets, with all the soviets then being controlled by the party.

Treatment of ethnic minorities

Early 1920s: ethnic minorities given rights and self-government, but under control of USSR.

⬇

Stalin, as Commissar for Nationalities, encouraged national cultures: e.g. languages.

⬇

Later 1920s: nationalism became a problem. Attempts to develop a Soviet nationalism.

⬇

1930s: Stalin suspects many non-Russian nationalities as being 'enemies of the people'.

⬇

1932–41: Purges of ethnic minorities; executions and forced exiles.

This poster from the 1930s shows Stalin in front of a map of the southern USSR (including Ukraine), surrounded by Soviet citizens of many different ethnicities. Stalin was himself from Georgia, not from Russia: one reason why Lenin appointed him as his Commissar for Nationalities. However, Stalin himself believed that the Russian nation was the best in the world.

Reasons for the persecution of ethnic minorities

Under Stalin, Soviet policy towards ethnic minorities changed radically.

- In the later 1920s, people began to be criticised for 'bourgeois nationalism': putting their ethnic identities first. Instead, Soviet nationalism was encouraged. People should be Soviet citizens, proud of the USSR.

- Resistance to collectivisation was often strongest where national identities were strongest. The terrible famine of 1932–33 that collectivisation created was blamed on Ukrainian nationalists.

- Stalin became convinced that some nationalities within the USSR were enemies of the people: a threat to the USSR. This was sometimes because of their ethnic link to other countries (e.g. Soviets with German ethnicity or Korean ethnicity), sometimes for different reasons (e.g. Civil War alliances).

Features of the persecution of ethnic minorities

From 1932, ethnic minorities became a target for the purges because of their suspected 'counter-revolutionary' tendencies. During the terror, the secret police had quotas for specific ethnic minorities, e.g. Polish or Chechen people.

In 1935–36, the purges targeted nationalities of the western USSR, e.g. Finns, Germans, Poles.

⮕

In 1937–38, 250 000 people were executed because of their national identity. 170 000 Soviet Koreans were exiled to Kazakhstan.

⮕

In 1941, hundreds of thousands of Soviet Germans were exiled to Siberia.

Think about the links some ethic minorities had with countries bordering the USSR

Now try this

Why did Stalin become suspicious of ethnic minorities?

Exam overview

This page introduces you to the main features and requirements of the Paper 3 Option 30 exam paper.

About Paper 3

- Paper 3 is for your modern depth study.
- Russia and the Soviet Union, 1917–41 is a modern depth study and is Option 30.
- It is divided into two sections: Section A and Section B. You must answer **all** questions in both sections.
- You will receive two documents: a question paper, which you write on, and a Sources/Interpretations Booklet, which you will need for Section B.

⏱ The Paper 3 exam lasts for 1 hour 20 minutes (80 minutes). There are 52 marks in total. You should spend approximately 25 minutes on Section A and 55 minutes on Section B.

You can see examples of all six questions on pages 33–38, and in the practice questions on pages 40–51.

The questions

The questions for Paper 3 will always follow this pattern:

Section A: Question 1

Give **two** things you can infer from Source A about …   **(4 marks)**

Complete the table.

Question 1 targets AO3 (analysing, evaluating and using sources to make judgements). Spend about six minutes on this question, which focuses on **inference** and **analysing** sources. Look out for the key term 'infer'.

Section A: Question 2

Explain why …   **(12 marks)**

Two prompts and your own information.

Question 2 targets both AO1 (showing knowledge and understanding of the topic) and AO2 (explaining and analysing events using historical concepts such as causation, consequences, change, continuity, similarity and difference). Spend approximately 18 minutes on this question.

Section B: Question 3(a)

How useful are Sources B and C for an enquiry into …?   **(8 marks)**

Use the sources and your knowledge of the historical context.

Question 3(a) also targets AO3. Spend about 12 minutes on this question, which is about **evaluating the usefulness** of contemporary sources.

Section B: Question 3(b)

Study Interpretations 1 and 2 …

What is the main difference between these views?   **(4 marks)**

Use details from both interpretations.

Questions 3(b) and 3(c) target AO4 (analysing, evaluating and making judgements about interpretations). Spend about six minutes on each of these questions, which are about **suggesting and explaining why** the interpretations differ.

Section B: Question 3(c)

Suggest **one** reason why Interpretations 1 and 2 give different views about …   **(4 marks)**

You can use the sources provided to help explain your answer.

Section B: Question 3(d)

How far do you agree with Interpretation 1/2 about …? **(16 marks + 4 marks for SpaG and use of specialist terminology)**

Question 3(d) also targets AO4. Spend about 30 minutes on this question, which is about **evaluating** an interpretation. Up to 4 marks are available for **spelling, punctuation, grammar (SPaG)** and use of specialist terminology.

Use both interpretations and your knowledge of the historical context.

Sources and interpretations

This exam asks you to analyse and evaluate both sources and interpretations, and you need different skills for each.

Questions 1 and 3(a)

Here you will be asked to look at sources. These sources could be propaganda posters, accounts from people at that time, photographs or any written or visual source that is **from the period**. As the sources are generated from that time it is helpful to think about the nature of the source, the origin, who produced it, and the purpose for which it was produced.

Questions 3(b), (c) and (d)

Here you will be asked to read interpretations of a particular enquiry or event from two different historians. Unlike analysing sources, interpretations are written **after the time period or event**. They are often written by historians or commentators who express their views and opinions about historical people, events and changes. As they are people's views and judgements based on evidence, there can be differences, and sometimes clear disagreements, about what people think.

Content: what information can you get directly from the source and its caption? It is important to spend time reading and studying sources before you read the exam questions.

Bias: a source is still useful even if you think it is biased – it can be good for assessing people's opinions of an event, for example.

Nature: what type of source is it – a diary entry, newspaper article, cartoon? This will help you to assess reliability, usefulness and purpose.

Language: in written sources, the author's language should give you clues about whether they are biased or even unreliable. Using appropriate examples by quoting directly from the source will help you gain better marks. Language can also tell you about the purpose of a source.

Hints and tips for examining sources

Origins: the caption should tell you who produced the source and when. The origin will help you assess its reliability, usefulness and purpose.

Purpose: the reason a source was created could be one of the questions by itself, but this will also help you to assess its reliability and usefulness.

Selection: what has the author/artist chosen to include? What have they chosen to leave out? It's important to consider both of these when you are thinking about the reliability, usefulness and purpose of a source.

Hints and tips for analysing and evaluating interpretations

How complete?	How objective?	What is the chosen emphasis?
The interpretations can be different because they are concerned with finding out about different aspects of the enquiry and may cover different ground. Sometimes historians set out to look at one aspect specifically, whereas others may want to look at related issues in a broader sense.	Historians can hold different views because they come from a particular school of thought. Therefore, their questions and answers are shaped by their wider views of society and how it works and has worked in the past. This can have an important impact on the judgements and opinions they hold about historical matters.	Sometimes, historians use the same sources but reach different views because they place a different level of importance on the same evidence. They may have access to the same material sources as each other, but will draw different conclusions about the significance of that evidence.

Question 1: Making inferences

Question 1 on your exam paper will ask you to 'infer from Source A ...'. There are 4 marks available for this question.

Source A: A Bolshevik poster from 1920. It says, 'Comrade Lenin cleans the world of rubbish', and shows him sweeping rulers, a priest and a capitalist away.

Тов. Ленин ОЧИЩАЕТ землю от нечисти.

Making inferences from a source

Making inferences is working something out that isn't directly shown. First of all, think about what is suggested or implied by the source and then try to show how the source helped you make that inference. Include supporting details from the source to back up what you say.

Worked example

Give **two** things you can infer from Source A about propaganda in Bolshevik Russia.

Complete the table below to explain your answer.

(4 marks)

 Links You can revise Soviet propaganda on pages 22–23.

Sample answer

(i) What I can infer:
That the Bolsheviks wanted ordinary people in Russia to see everyone who used to be in charge of tsarist Russia as being 'rubbish'.

Details in the source that tell me this:
The way Lenin is shown sweeping the little figures away. The caption that talks about cleaning rubbish.

(ii) What I can infer:
That while the old rulers of Russia were wealthy capitalists, Lenin was an ordinary person, a worker, like most people in Russia.

Details in the source that tell me this:
Lenin is shown wearing an ordinary person's hat and sweeping like an ordinary person would. The old rulers are shown as fat – they were greedy people who made themselves rich from ordinary people's work.

You must consider the intended audience and the purpose for which the source was produced. Also, think about when it was produced as this context is vital for analysing the source, not just describing it.

 Sometimes, it is helpful to think about what you can see and then move on to think about what it **suggests**. You need to make sure that you don't just describe the source but go further and show you can make inferences.

Question 2: Explaining causes

Question 2 on your exam paper will ask you to 'Explain why ...'. There are 12 marks available for this question.

Worked example

Explain why Stalin was able to win the struggle for power that followed Lenin's death. **(12 marks)**

You may use the following in your answer:

- Trotsky
- control of party administration.

You **must** also use information of your own.

Explaining key features and causes

Explaining why involves looking at the key features of something and thinking about its causes. Key features are accurate and relevant knowledge. Causes are what led to a situation or change happening. To explain causes, you must show how a number of causes led to that event or change.

 You can revise the struggle for power on page 19.

You **must** use your own knowledge and not limit yourself to the bullet points.

Sample extract

Stalin was able to win the struggle for power because of Trotsky's weaknesses, even though Trotsky had been very important in the Revolution and led the Bolshevik Civil War victory.

Stalin was also the General Secretary of the party. This helped him win the struggle for power because it gave him control.

 Here the student has given a correct cause but only given a vague answer and doesn't develop an explanation.

This is also a correct cause and the beginning of an explanation: the student needs to add more detail to the explanation to improve this answer.

Improved extract

After Lenin died, most people expected Trotsky to succeed Lenin as leader because he had led the Bolsheviks to victory in the Civil War and had been Lenin's right hand man during the October Revolution. One reason for Stalin's rise to power was that Stalin exploited Trotsky's weaknesses in order to remove him as a rival. Trotsky was arrogant and, because he had only joined the Bolsheviks (from the Mensheviks) in 1917, he did not have a core of support in the party. Because Trotsky was expected to take over from Lenin, all the other rivals were happy to join with Stalin in opposing Trotsky and criticising his views, for example the Left Communist support for Permanent Revolution.

Because of Stalin's control of party organisation, he was able, along with Zinoviev and Kamenev, to ensure that crucial votes went against Trotsky at the 1925 Party Congress.

Stalin's position as General Secretary of the party was another important cause.

 Make sure you identify reasons that help 'explain why' rather than writing descriptions of events.

 Link your answer to the question as this student has done with the phrase: 'One reason for Stalin's rise to power ...'

 Use your knowledge of the period to support your answer with specific information.

 The information about Stalin's rise to power shows use of relevant knowledge. Revise these points on page 19.

 Using phrases like 'was another important cause' to add a new point is a good way of writing a clear answer.

Question 3(a): Evaluating usefulness

Question 3(a) on your exam paper will ask you to judge 'How useful are Sources B and C ...'. There are 8 marks available for this question.

Worked example

Study Sources B and C on page 39.

How useful are Sources B and C for an enquiry into why the February Revolution succeeded in overthrowing tsarism?

Explain your answer, using Sources B and C and your knowledge of the historical context. **(8 marks)**

Judging usefulness of sources

To judge the usefulness of a source, you need to think about the enquiry question and the criteria you will use to reach your decision. You will need to consider the **provenance** of each source – its nature, origin and purpose – and whether these make the source useful or not in addressing the enquiry question.

 **Links** You can revise the February Revolution on pages 3–4.

Sample extract

Source C is useful because it is written by the governor of Petrograd at the time of the revolution. He says that the February Revolution 'was a total defeat for us' because the people could tell that the army and the government were scared of them.

 This answer lacks analysis and describes rather than judges the usefulness of the sources.

Improved extract

Source C is more useful because it is written by the man who was governor of Petrograd in February 1917. It was written over ten years after the revolution, in a memoir, and the writer might have misremembered some details or might have worried about what people would think of him. This could limit its usefulness, but I think not too much because what Source C describes is the honest recognition by the governor that he had lost control of Petrograd and that a 'total defeat' followed. Source C also provides the valuable insight from the governor about the military decision to fire on the crowds: the governor saw this as a critical mistake, which had significant impacts not only on the crowds, but also on the army. Source C's judgement seems to be that the 'total defeat' happened when soldiers joined the crowds in protest.

 This student has used criteria about origins and audience in judging the usefulness of this source for the enquiry.

 Use specific language in your answer. Here the student has used vocabulary such as: limit, insight, critical, impacts, judgement.

Key terms

Provenance – the origin of a source.
Nature – what type of source it is, such as a propaganda poster or a speech extract.
Purpose – the reason a source was created.

 This is a good answer because it evaluates Source C for this enquiry by considering its **nature** and **purpose**.

Question 3(b): Identifying and explaining differences

Question 3(b) on your exam paper will ask you to identify 'the main differences between the views' in two interpretations. There are 4 marks available for this question.

Worked example

Study Interpretations 1 and 2 on page 39. They give different views about who led the February Revolution.

What is the main difference between these views?

Explain your answer, using details from both interpretations. **(4 marks)**

Remember to include points from **both** interpretations. It's important to refer directly to the interpretation and include short quotations to support what you say.

Spotting and explaining differences in interpretations

An interpretation is a historian's account or explanation based on evidence. When analysing the differences between interpretations, think about the points of view the historians present. Look for the important or key differences, not just the surface details. For this question you need to look for a fundamental difference that you can spot.

 Links For more information about the February Revolution, see pages 3–4.

Sample answer

These interpretations are different because the first one says that no one really knows who the leaders of the February Revolution were while the second one does know who they were: the Bolsheviks and the Mensheviks and SRs.

 This answer focuses on a surface point of difference rather than the underlying difference. A stronger answer would pick out a more fundamental difference.

Improved answer

 Use short quotations to support your analysis.

Figes argues that the revolutionary parties, the Bolsheviks, Mensheviks and SRs, were not the leaders of the February Revolution – they were all 'caught unawares'. Instead, he claims that the February Revolution was led, if it was led at all, by lots of different ordinary people.

Make sure the focus of your answer is on the key point of difference rather than more minor differences.

The Soviet account in Interpretation 2 argues against this view. It states that the Bolsheviks were the leaders of the revolution on the streets. While Figes does say that some of the people leading on the streets were 'socialists', Interpretation 2 implies that the Bolshevik Party had decided to take an active role in leading the February Revolution and were working to an agreed plan. This is contradicted by Figes in Interpretation 1 because he points out that the leaders of the Bolshevik Party were all in 'exile, in prison or abroad', making it impossible for the Bolsheviks to 'directly lead' the revolution as Interpretation 2 implies.

 You need to explain a key difference and support your explanation with detailed points from **both** interpretations.

 You must think about the specific language you can use in your answer like: 'argues', 'claims', 'states', 'implies' and 'This is contradicted ...'. These phrases help you to produce a better answer because they help to show you are analysing another person's judgement or opinion about something.

Question 3(c): Suggesting reasons for different views

Question 3(c) on your exam paper will ask you to explain why two interpretations give different views. There are 4 marks for this question.

Worked example

Suggest **one** reason why Interpretations 1 and 2 on page 39 give different views about leadership in the February Revolution.

You may use Sources B and C on page 39 to help explain your answer.   **(4 marks)**

You must give **one** reason why historians reach different conclusions about historical questions.

'Suggest' questions

In a question that asks you to suggest a reason, you need to offer and explain an idea about why there are differences. You need to show you understand that historical interpretations are judgements and opinions based on evidence and that, as a result, different views can exist.

Links You can revise Bolshevik involvement in the February Revolution on page 4.

Sample answer

The Soviet Union was based on the idea that the Bolshevik Party had led the workers in a socialist revolution. It would have been politically embarrassing for the Soviet Union to admit that the Bolshevik leadership was taken by surprise by the February Revolution, and that it had very little influence on what soldiers, workers and peasants did to overthrow the tsarist government. This is why Interpretation 2 stresses that the Bolsheviks 'were directly leading the struggle of the masses in the streets', even though the Bolshevik leaders were exiled or in prison.

Modern historians, like Figes in Interpretation 1, do not have to follow an official line like the Soviet-era historians had to do. They are free to make their own interpretations based on what the sources tell them. Interpretation 2 was written only 20 years after the February Revolution and had a very tight focus: the official 'History of the Communist Party of the Soviet Union'. Interpretation 1, in contrast, was published nearly a hundred years after the February Revolution, which meant it could be informed by much more research and by an understanding of what happened to the USSR.

 In this answer, the explanation of the differences looks at the different focus chosen by each historian.

 You can use detail from the sources to support your argument about why the interpretations differ – here, the main difference being the ideological bias behind Interpretation 2.

 Make sure the explanation in your answer is clear and refers to **both** interpretations.

 Take the **context** of why and when the interpretations were written into account when you explain the differences between them.

Question 3(d): Evaluating interpretations

Question 3(d) on your exam paper will ask you to evaluate an interpretation by explaining how far you agree with it. There are 16 marks available for this question. An additional 4 marks are available for good spelling, punctuation and grammar (SPaG) and use of historical terminology.

Worked example

How far do you agree with Interpretation 2 on page 39 about the leadership of the February Revolution of 1917?

Explain your answer, using both interpretations and your knowledge of the historical context.

(16 marks plus 4 marks for SPaG and use of specialist terminology)

 Links Find out more about the leadership of the February Revolution on page 4.

How far do you agree?

You must:

- ✓ explore different views on the debate
- ✓ reach a clear judgement yourself
- ✓ give detailed knowledge of the context and wider issues
- ✓ use both interpretations, not just the one stated in the question
- ✓ explain your answer – develop and give reasons.

Sample extract

I don't agree with the interpretation that the Bolsheviks were responsible for leading the protests in the streets. I think this was more to do with Soviet propaganda rather than historically accurate research. It is true that the Mensheviks and SRs got control of the Petrograd Soviet, as Interpretation 2 says, but the interpretation seems to be annoyed about this instead of pleased about other revolutionary parties being involved.

A clear view is given in this answer with a supporting reason.

A point is made by the student but there is no supporting evidence. Only one interpretation is referenced.

The student attempts to develop a line of argument but it is not well chosen because the student hasn't properly understood the Bolsheviks' problems with Mensheviks and SRs.

Improved extract

I do not agree with Interpretation 2 that the Bolsheviks were 'directly leading the struggle of the masses in the streets' because this goes against the historical evidence that the February Revolution was spontaneous, arising from popular unrest about food prices and the war. I agree more on this point with Figes (Interpretation 1) that the 'street generated its own leaders'.

I do agree more with Interpretation 2's claims about the Petrograd Soviet, though not with what it goes on to say about the war aims of the Mensheviks and SRs: I feel this is Soviet propaganda against their political rivals who were, in 1938, being purged in the Great Terror. The Mensheviks and SRs did dominate the Petrograd Soviet, and this was due partly to the absence of exiled and imprisoned Bolshevik leaders. However, I think that the main reason was that workers and peasants agreed with the Mensheviks and SRs. This is supported by the results of the Constituent Assembly in 1917, which was dominated by votes for SRs.

Highlighting key points in the interpretation can help you focus on the precise arguments that you need to evaluate to make your judgement.

You need to evaluate different points made by the interpretations while putting your arguments in a wider context.

Remember that for this question 4 marks are available for good spelling, grammar, punctuation and use of historical terminology. Use specific historical vocabulary, such as: Mensheviks, SRs, Petrograd Soviet, propaganda, purged, Constituent Assembly.

Sources/Interpretations Booklet

These sources and interpretations are referred to in the worked examples on pages 35–38.

Source B: A photograph from February 1917 showing armed Petrograd civilians marching with army mutineers (soldiers who had rebelled against the army authorities).

Source C: From the memoirs of A.P. Balk, Governor of Petrograd in February 1917, which were written in 1929.

February 25 was a total defeat for us. Not only were the leaders of the revolutionary action convinced that the troops were acting without spirit, even unwillingly, but the crowd also sensed the weakness of the authorities and became emboldened. The decision of the military authorities to impose control by force, in exceptional circumstances to use arms, not only poured oil on the fire but shook up the troops and allowed them to think that the authorities … feared 'the people'.

Interpretation 1: From *Revolutionary Russia, 1891–1991* by Orlando Figes, published in 2014.

There was no real leadership on the people's side. The socialist parties were all caught unawares, their main leaders in exile, in prison or abroad … The street generated its own leaders – students, workers, cadets …, socialists whose names have never made it into history books.

Interpretation 2: From *The History of the CPSU* (Communist Party of the Soviet Union), published in 1938, which provides a Soviet account of the February Revolution in 1917.

While the Bolsheviks were directly leading the struggle of the masses in the streets, the compromising parties, the Mensheviks and Socialist-Revolutionaries, were seizing the seats in the Soviets and building up a majority there. This was partly facilitated by the fact that the majority of the leaders of the Bolshevik Party were in prison or exile … while the Mensheviks and Socialist-Revolutionaries were freely promenading the streets of Petrograd … The Socialist-Revolutionaries and Mensheviks had not the slightest intention of [ending] the war, of securing peace …

Practice

Put your skills and knowledge into practice with the following question.

Option 30: Russia and the Soviet Union, 1917–41

SECTION A

Answer questions 1 and 2.

Source A: From a speech by Stalin at the first All-Union Conference of Stakhanovites, 17 November 1935.

> And, indeed, look at our comrades, the Stakhanovites, more closely. What type of people are they?
>
> They are mostly young or middle-aged working men and women, people with culture and technical knowledge, who show examples of precision and accuracy in work, who are able to appreciate the time factor in work, and who have learned to count not only the minutes, but also the seconds. … They are free of the conservatism and stagnation of certain engineers, technicians and business executives; … they often supplement and correct what the engineers and technicians have to say, they often teach them and impel them forward, for they are people who have completely mastered the technique of their job, and who are able to squeeze out of technique the maximum that can be squeezed out of it.

1 Give **two** things you can infer from Source A about why Stalin promoted the idea of Stakhanovites.

Complete the table below to explain your answer.

(4 marks)

(i) What I can infer:

 Guided   Stalin said that the Stakhanovites were people who had 'completely mastered' their jobs in every detail.

This suggests that ....

Details in the source that tell me this:

....

....

....

(ii) What I can infer:

....

....

....

Details in the source that tell me this:

....

....

....

You have 1 hour 20 minutes for the **whole** of Paper 3, so you should use the time carefully to answer all the questions fully. Remember to leave 5 minutes or so to check your work when you've finished writing.

Links You can revise Stakhanovites on page 26.

Spend about 6 minutes on this answer. You need to identify **two** valid inferences from the source.

To 'infer' is to make a claim based on evidence, in this case the source you are given in the exam.

An example of a suitable inference might be that 'I can infer that Stalin wanted to promote Stakhanovites because he made a speech to a Stakhanovite conference in 1935.'

You need to give supporting details selected from the source to back up both your inferences.

Practice

Put your skills and knowledge into practice with the following question.

2 Explain why the Bolsheviks were able to win the Civil War, 1918–21.

You may use the following in your answer:

- Trotsky's appointment as war commissar in March 1918
- the lack of a single White leader.

You **must** also use information of your own.   **(12 marks)**

Guided   There are a number of reasons why the Bolsheviks

were able to win the Civil War in 1921.

....

....

....

....

....

....

....

....

....

....

....

....

....

....

....

....

....

....

....

....

....

....

You have 1 hour 20 minutes for the **whole** of Paper 3, so spend about 18 minutes on this answer.

'Explain' means you have to give reasons for the Bolshevik victory, not just describe what happened in the Civil War.

You need to include information of your own that is not in the bullet point hints.

Links   You can revise the Civil War on pages 12–13.

Marks are awarded for your analysis and understanding of causation and for your knowledge and understanding of the topic.

Useful phrases when answering causation questions include: because, led to, resulted in, reasons for, factors that caused.

Keep your explanations focused on the question. Although you might remember lots of detail about the Civil War, you need to focus on providing reasons why the Bolsheviks were able to win.

Practice

Use this page to continue your answer to question 2.

....

....

....

....

....

....

....

....

....

....

....

....

....

....

....

....

....

....

....

....

....

....

....

....

....

You need to show a good knowledge of the key features and characteristics of the event and analyse causation. You also need to show how factors combine to bring about an outcome – in this case, how different factors came together, resulting in the Bolshevik victory.

Practice

Use this page to continue your answer to question 2.

....

....

....

....

....

....

....

....

....

....

....

....

....

....

....

....

....

....

....

....

....

....

....

....

....

....

You must include a conclusion to sum up how the different causes led to this event.

Practice

Put your skills and knowledge into practice with the following question.

SECTION B

3 (a) Study Sources B and C on page 52.

How useful are Sources B and C for an enquiry into public reactions to the show trials of 1936–1938?

Explain your answer, using Sources B and C and your knowledge of the historical context.   **(8 marks)**

You should spend about 12 minutes on this answer.

'How useful' means you have to judge what the sources suggest about the enquiry question and what the limits or problems could be.

Guided   Both Sources B and C are useful for finding out about how ordinary people reacted to the show trials.

....

....

....

....

....

....

Links You can revise the show trials of 1936–38 on page 21.

....

....

....

....

....

....

....

You need to identify and comment on the pros and cons of each of the sources and make a judgement.

....

....

....

....

....

....

Make sure you include some knowledge of the context and don't just rely on information given in the sources.

....

....

....

....

....

Practice

Use this page to continue your answer to question 3(a).

Guided   However, there are some drawbacks with both

sources for this enquiry. For example,

....

....

....

....

....

....

....

....

....

....

....

....

....

....

....

....

....

....

....

....

....

....

....

....

Remember, you need to evaluate the usefulness of both sources.

Practice

Put your skills and knowledge into practice with the following question.

3 (b) Study Interpretations 1 and 2 on page 53. They give different views about Stalin and the terror between 1936 and 1938.

What is the main difference between these views?

Explain your answer, using details from both interpretations. **(4 marks)**

 You should spend about six minutes on this answer.

 Links You can revise the use of terror in the 1930s on page 21.

Guided Interpretations 1 and 2 both discuss the terror

....

but offer different views about Stalin's role.

....

....

....

....

....

....

....

....

....

 You need to identify the key difference, rather than just surface differences.

 Make sure you refer to **both** the interpretations.

 Remember, historians' interpretations are **their** views and opinions about causes, events and significance.

 Remember to focus on the underlying **difference**.

Practice

Put your skills and knowledge into practice with the following question.

3 (c) Suggest **one** reason why Interpretations 1 and 2 on page 53 give different views about Stalin's role in the terror between 1936 and 1938.

You may use Sources B and C on page 52 to help explain your answer. **(4 marks)**

 You should spend about six minutes on this answer.

 You need to explain **one** reason why the interpretations differ.

Guided   Interpretations 1 and 2 offer different views

....

because

....

....

....

....

....

....

....

....

....

....

You can revise how to analyse interpretations on page 32.

 Make sure you refer to **both** the interpretations to back up your answer.

 Remember, historians' interpretations are **their** views and opinions about causes, events and significance.

 Remember to explain either the historians' focus, emphasis or the different weight they give to the sources.

Practice

Put your skills and knowledge into practice with the following question.

Up to 4 marks of the total will be awarded for spelling, punctuation, grammar and use of specialist terminology.

3 (d) How far do you agree with Interpretation 1 on page 53 about Stalin's role in the terror between 1936 and 1938?

Explain your answer, using both interpretations and your knowledge of the historical context. **(20 marks)**

Guided | .... with the views in Interpretation 1

....

....

....

....

....

....

....

....

....

....

....

....

....

....

....

....

....

....

....

....

....

....

You should spend about 30 minutes on this answer.

You can revise how to analyse and evaluate interpretations on page 32.

You need to provide a clear line of argument. Say whether you agree or disagree in the first sentence.

Say why you think the interpretation is valid or questionable.

Remember that 4 marks are for **SPaG** in this question. Make sure you leave time to check your spelling, punctuation and grammar.

Make sure you refer clearly to your **own knowledge** of the historical context.

Practice

Use this page to continue your answer to question 3(d).

Remember, historians' interpretations offer **their** views for you to challenge.

Make sure you refer to **both** the interpretations to back up your answer.

Include a number of reasons for your opinion to build an argument throughout.

Practice

Use this page to continue your answer to question 3(d).

Practice

Use this page to continue your answer to question 3(d).

....

....

.... ← Include a brief conclusion to sum up your argument.

....

....

....

....

....

....

....

....

....

....

....

....

....

....

....

....

....

....

....

....

....

....

....

Sources/Interpretations Booklet 1

Sources B and C for use with the Section B questions on pages 44–51.

Source B: A photo from 1937 which shows workers at the Dynamo factory in Moscow voting for the execution of Zinoviev and other 'Trotskyites' following a show trial.

Source C: From a letter written in 1936 by a Soviet citizen to the head of the Party commission responsible for uncovering Trotskyites within Soviet society.

On reading in the paper the charges against the fascist hirelings L. Trotsky, Zinoviev and Co., I could not react calmly – I just do not know how to express my outrage – I felt such hatred towards these scoundrels that I fell to thinking about how all honest Party and non-Party Bolsheviks should keep an eye on their friends and acquaintance: how they breathe, how they live and what they do, in order to completely unmask all traces of Zinovievism – and there are plenty, I suspect.

Sources/Interpretations Booklet 2

Interpretations 1 and 2 for use with Section B questions on pages 44–51.

Interpretation 1: From *Stalin's Russia 1924–1953* by Robin Bunce and Laura Gallagher, published in 2008.

> At the end of 1934 Stalin launched a wave of political terror that claimed a million lives and resulted in twelve million people being sent to forced-labour camps. … Stalin's paranoia led to the Great Terror, because he felt unable to trust many within the Communist Party and therefore acted to remove those he saw as potential threats.

Interpretation 2: From *The Soviet Union: A Very Short Introduction* by Stephen Lovell, published in 2009.

> How could a society have succumbed [given in] to this madness? How could it have ended up seeing enemies everywhere?
>
> Stalin was probably the only person to understand the full scale of what was happening [in the Great Terror], and he was certainly the only person who could have brought it to an end …. But even Stalin was sending out signals rather than directing every stage of the terror process: and even he seems to have been surprised (though not displeased) by the scale and intensity of the violence. … It was as if all members of Soviet society were guilty until proved innocent – and innocence could not be proved once and for all.

Answers

Where an exemplar answer has been provided, it does not necessarily represent the only correct response. In most cases there are a range of responses that can gain full marks.

SUBJECT CONTENT
The revolutions of 1917
Russia in early 1917
1. Threats to the tsarist regime

The liberal parties did not want the social tensions in Russia to erupt into another revolution, like that of 1905, but they still wanted to achieve wide-ranging social reforms that would have severely limited the power of the tsar and made Russia into a constitutional democracy. This would have enabled everyone's rights to be protected in law and written down in a constitution, rather than a police state as Russia had become under the tsarist regime, and with the laws made by an elected parliament rather than by the tsar alone. The tsarist regime was an autocratic system in which all power in the Russian Empire belonged to the tsar. It was not compatible with what the liberals wanted to see Russia become.

2. The First World War

This was an attack on the tsar because he had taken over as commander-in-chief of the army, and therefore the incompetence that affected the military campaign (for example, the fact that one-third of soldiers had no rifles in 1915) was ultimately the tsar's responsibility. The words 'evil intentions' could be an attack on Tsarina Alexandra because, as a German, she was suspected of trying to engineer a German victory against Russia.

The February Revolution
3. Triggers for revolt

- The tsar being away from Petrograd: the tsar left Petrograd to return to army headquarters in Mogilev on 22 February. This contributed to the February Revolution because it meant the tsar wasn't in Petrograd to take charge of the situation and possibly rally his troops to prevent the mutiny.
- Contempt for the tsarina: Alexandra was mistrusted as a German and despised or ridiculed for her dependence on Rasputin. This contempt contributed to the February Revolution by undermining the authority of the tsar and the legitimacy of the royal family's position of autocratic power.
- The army's mutiny: this took place from 26 February when troops began to refuse to fire on demonstrators, and spread as more regiments joined in the mutiny, with some soldiers giving guns to the demonstrators. This contributed to the revolution significantly, as the tsarist government depended on the army and police to keep Petrograd under control.
- Unusually mild winter weather: Petrograd in February was usually too cold for people to stay on the streets for long. The unusually mild weather contributed to the February Revolution because it meant that thousands more people joined in the demonstrations.
- Demonstrations in support of the Duma, the International Women's Day March and the industrial unrest all brought men and women on to the streets in marches and demonstrations, which led to clashes with the police and to revolution.
- The announcement of possible bread rationing, coming on top of a winter of food shortages, made people desperate. This contributed to the February Revolution as it showed people they had nothing to lose.

4. The abdication of the tsar

It is useful in that it is from Nicholas himself and gives some insight into Nicholas' state of mind in the days leading up to his abdication. This diary entry suggests Nicholas was in denial about the revolution – he avoids spending much time listening to reports of the revolution (even though he complains before that the news is only fragmentary: i.e. in bits and pieces), and goes for walks instead, noting the weather. He appears quite mild: his own troops are mutinying against his government and he calls it 'unfortunate'. However, he is also frustrated at being so far away: as we know, the tsar did try to get back to Petrograd. The quote suggests that Nicholas did recognise that he was not able to do anything in the situation and that, once the army stopped doing as he ordered, he actually had little power at all. This makes it useful for arguments that Nicholas was feeling hopeless and powerless when he was asked to abdicate.

The Provisional Government
5. The Provisional Government

The liberals, who wanted more political freedoms, gained most because the Provisional Government was committed to setting up elections for a democratic government for the Russian Republic: the Constituent Assembly.

6. Weaknesses and failures

'Order Number 1' undermined the authority of the Provisional Government because the Order said that the army and navy would only obey orders from the Provisional Government if those orders were also approved by the Petrograd Soviet. Instead of the Provisional Government being able to make decisions and command the armed forces to act, the government had to get the agreement of the Petrograd Soviet first. 'Order Number 1' also specified that regiments would now be responsible for discipline and that this would be carried out by councils of ordinary soldiers, not by the officers who were under the command of the Provisional Government. This completely undermined the authority of the officers, making their lives very difficult (and dangerous) and losing their respect for the Provisional Government.

7. The Kornilov Revolt

Reasons could include one of the following:

- Kornilov wanted order and authority in Russia, which Dual Power was not delivering.
- He saw the Bolsheviks and the Petrograd Soviet as having a destabilising effect on the Russian Empire – the soviets were undermining the authority of the government to govern Russia. The soviets had undermined the authority of army officers to command their men.
- Kerensky had known about and agreed with Kornilov's plan, so he thought he was acting with the support of the Provisional Government.

The Bolshevik Revolution
8. Lenin's return

The soviets were local-level councils that had sprung up in different parts of the Russian Republic to organise local government, to manage factories and administer rural districts. Lenin believed these soviets were socialist and showed how a socialist country could be run. Instead of having general elections for a government to run Russia, with an elected parliament to make laws, Lenin said Russia was ready to go straight to a socialist way of running the country, by giving all the power to govern Russia to the soviets.

9. The Bolsheviks seize power

There is no doubt that the Provisional Government was very unpopular by the time of the October 1917 Revolution because of food shortages, rationing and unemployment, as well as the state of the economy in towns and cities (and peasant discontent about land ownership in the country). But the October Revolution was different in several ways from earlier uprisings against the failures of the Provisional Government. This time, Lenin did not join in an existing wave of protests against the government. Instead Lenin and Trotsky carefully organised a way to grab power from the Provisional Government. The October Revolution was carried out by a relatively small number of loyal Bolsheviks. It succeeded because the Provisional Government was very weak. If the Provisional Government had been more popular, Kerensky might have been able to organise a defence against the Bolsheviks. But the October Revolution did not succeed just because the Provisional Government was unpopular. There were plenty of people who did not support the Provisional Government who also did not want the Bolsheviks to get into power: for example, many of the other socialist parties in the Petrograd Soviet.

The Bolsheviks in power, 1917–24
Consolidation of power, 1917–18
10. Early decrees and execution of the tsar

The elections to the Constituent Assembly were won by the Socialist Revolutionaries (SRs), with 53 per cent of the vote (21.8 million votes and 410 seats in the Constituent Assembly). Although the SRs were socialists like the Bolsheviks, they had different ideas about how Russia should be run and would not have allowed the Bolsheviks or the soviet system to remain in charge. If Lenin wanted to keep control of Russia, he therefore could not accept the result of the Constituent Assembly elections.

Another reason was that Lenin felt the Constituent Assembly was a step backwards for socialism in Russia: Russia had developed the soviet system, which was much more socialist than parliamentary democracy because it was run by the workers themselves. However, this is not a very convincing reason because a) Lenin had supported elections for the Constituent Assembly when doing this was a good way of criticising the Provisional Government, and b) Lenin had already begun to sideline the soviets and rule Russia through the Council of People's Commissars, which was controlled by the Bolsheviks, with Lenin as the chair.

11. The Treaty of Brest-Litovsk

One of the reasons why the Bolsheviks agreed to sign the Treaty of Brest-Litovsk, despite the terrible losses it meant to Russia, was the belief that further socialist revolutions in the other European countries fighting the First World War were inevitable. Trotsky thought the harsh terms of the treaty would appal the German workers who would see that their leaders hated the thought of proletarians in control of a country. This would make the German workers rise up in revolution. Once other countries joined Russia in socialism, it wouldn't matter whose territory used to belong to whom.

The Civil War, 1918–21
12. The Civil War

The Mensheviks and SRs wanted to rule within the Constitutional Assembly as an elected government. However, Lenin increasingly ignored the soviets and wanted to show the Mensheviks and SRs that the Bolsheviks were no longer interested in sharing power with them, but also that the Bolsheviks were not going to give up power to anyone, not even the workers. Towards the end of the Civil War, workers began to criticise the Bolsheviks for the same reason, saying that the Bolsheviks had created a new class of bureaucrats who had all the power and privileges in Russian society, while the workers were just as much slaves to the system as they had been under the tsarist regime.

13. The Bolshevik victory

Trotsky recognised that the Red Army needed experienced military specialists, and these were all former tsarist army officers. One way in which the commissars – Bolshevik political officers – were important was that they made sure that the ex-tsarist officers were never out of their sight: that way the specialists could never betray the Bolsheviks. Commissars provided Bolshevik political supervision at every rank (level) of the Red Army. The commissars were just as important as the military commander of a unit, and they could cancel orders given by the commander if they were not in accordance with Bolshevik strategy or aims. That gave the Bolsheviks very strong control over the army.

Moves towards totalitarianism
14. The Red Terror and the Cheka

The Cheka were the Bolsheviks' secret police. They helped the Bolsheviks keep power by crushing any political opposition. During the Civil War the Cheka was the leading force in the Red Terror, which arrested 87 000 people and shot 8389 of them. Not only did this remove actual political opponents of the Bolsheviks, it also removed people who were suspected of opposition and scared almost everyone else into doing what the Bolsheviks said.

15. Bolshevik centralisation

Lenin, as leader of both the Communist Party and the Sovnarkom, was able to unite the two to create a centralised government that became a dictatorship.

Economic and social change, 1918–24
16. War Communism

The Bolsheviks did obtain an end to Russia's involvement in the First World War, but the Treaty of Brest-Litovsk was a major cause of the Civil War, so peace was not achieved. The peasants had received land from the Bolsheviks, but under War Communism they had to hand over their crops to the government, leaving many desperately short of food. Bread was the Bolsheviks' promise to end food shortages, but under War Communism, food production crashed so badly that shortages became even worse.

17. New Economic Policy (NEP)

War Communism was a very strict form of communism in which state control took from everyone and gave back the most to those who were doing the most for the state: the Red Army in particular. There was no market for food – the state took food from the peasants and left them just a small amount to live on. The state took complete control of industry and organised it to make what the state needed to win the war. Strikes were banned. The state also used the Cheka to eliminate opposition and to try to make all the people committed to serving the state above their own interests.

The impact of all this was that the Bolsheviks won the Civil War, but at a high cost, including the Kronstadt Mutiny. NEP was a reluctant step back from communism: it reintroduced a market for food and stopped taking food from the peasants; it returned small factories to private ownership and allowed the manufacture of goods for profit. Money came back in, and anyone could start a shop and sell products for profit.

18. Social changes

One reason was that the Bolsheviks had set themselves up initially as leading the revolution on behalf of the proletariat, until such time as the proletariat could take over completely at which point the state would 'wither away' (disappear). This would only happen when the proletariat was politically educated: conscious (awake) to their destiny to take the USSR forward to being fully communist. A second, less theoretical, reason was that peasants and workers were more likely to support the Communist Party if they could read and understand Communist Party propaganda and Communist Party ideas. It was also the case that people had been deprived of education under tsarism and there was a real hunger for learning and an opportunity to better oneself, which fitted closely with communist ideas about the party's role in improving conditions for the working classes.

Stalin's rise to power and dictatorship, 1924–41
The struggle for power, 1924–28
19. Stalin leads the USSR

As General Secretary, Stalin was in charge of who were offered jobs in the Communist Party and he made sure he appointed people who would support him to the top posts. He was responsible for the 'Lenin Enrolment', which allowed many more workers into the Communist Party. These party members remained very loyal to Stalin in gratitude for this help, which gave them access to privileged positions in the USSR.

Unlike Trotsky, who had joined the Bolsheviks later than other senior Bolsheviks like Stalin, Stalin had used his position to develop many allies through the party. He was also careful as General Secretary to appear as a moderate, someone in the 'centre' of party politics rather than on the left or right wings of the party. Lenin had also not been General Secretary, which meant people underestimated the role and underestimated Stalin. This meant Stalin was able to arrange alliances against first one rival for power, and then another. Stalin's control of the party organisation meant that votes at the Party Congress could be guaranteed to go against his rivals. When Zinoviev and Kamenev formed the United Opposition with Trotsky, Stalin was able, from the centre of the party, to denounce them as factionalists – factionalism was something Lenin had expressly forbidden in the party.

Terror in the 1930s
20. The purges

The purges had a wide range of effects: around a million people were killed and about 8 million people were put in prison/forced labour camps. This meant that most of the survivors knew someone who was purged and that created an atmosphere of fear and suspicion among the whole population – since few of the people arrested had ever appeared to be traitors before. As well as fear of being surrounded by hidden traitors, some people also distrusted the secret police (although few people thought that Stalin was to blame) and the justice system. The loss of so many people meant skills were lost at all levels, especially in the army and the Communist Party, from industry and from agriculture. No one dared to criticise Stalin and this meant any mistakes he made were never challenged.

21. The NKVD, Gulag and show trials

By forcing former colleagues of Lenin, like Bukharin, to confess publicly to having committed 'monstrous' crimes of treachery against the Soviet Union, Stalin could convince Soviet citizens that there were enemies of the people at work against the USSR, at the very highest levels. The words the accused, like Bukharin, were made to say at their show trials also stressed the achievements of the USSR, to show that the enemies of the people had not been able to seriously damage the country. They were also made to praise Stalin, and the show trials were designed to reveal to people that only Stalin, of all Lenin's old colleagues, was able to defend the country against its enemies both abroad and at home.

Propaganda and censorship
22. Official culture and the new Constitution

Answers could include any three of the following:

- Without any other sources of information, lots of people did believe what they read and saw. Otherwise, they had to believe some very difficult things about the country they lived in.

- Not everyone believed what they were told, however. In public they acted as though they did believe the propaganda but in secret, with their most trusted friends, they criticised the regime. There was a saying in the USSR, for example, 'They pretend to pay us, and we pretend to work' – the consequence was very low productivity among workers.

- Although propaganda stressed the great achievements of the USSR and the horrors of capitalism, when Soviet soldiers fought in European countries in the Second World War they could see that actually people in other countries had far better lives than them.

- Fear of arrest and punishment meant that people sometimes behaved in ways that did not help improve living conditions in the USSR. For example, when sofa production was measured in the weight of sofas produced, Soviet manufacturers made each sofa as heavy as possible.

- Limited education, which repeated propaganda claims and discouraged alternative ways of thinking, meant many people didn't have the confidence to question the truth and so accepted what they were told.

- It was difficult to check any facts so it was easier just to accept them.

23. The cult of Stalin

For example:

- Stalin was referred to in semi-religious language: the sort of way that a saint or god would be described in some religions.

- Stalin assumed (took on) a tradition from the Russian tsars: the tsar as the peasants' 'little father', far away in Moscow but still caring for all his people as a father does his children.

Economic and social changes, 1924–41
Agriculture and collectivisation
24. Collectivisation

There was opposition from peasants to Stalin's policy of collectivisation so the Red Army was brought in to put pressure on peasants to work on the collective farms. With continued resistance, many peasants were killed or exiled to Siberia and their land seized.

25. Collectivisation: successes and failures

To answer this question you would need to consider a selection of collectivisation's successes and weigh them up against its failures, then come to a decision about the question which is supported by your analysis of the successes and failures. For example, one key success was getting almost all the USSR's peasantry into collective farms so rapidly: 90 per cent by 1935. However, the violent way in which this was done meant death or terrible suffering for many millions of peasants. This would surely outweigh the achievement of a high rate of collectivisation: the ends did not justify the means.

A second key success was industrialisation itself, which was only possible because the state could control collective farms so that workers could have very cheap food to eat. But this happened at the expense of the peasants, even to the point of taking so much from them that they had nothing to live on and nothing to grow for the following year, resulting in terrible famine in Ukraine and other regions.

Changes in industry
26. Industrialisation

Key features of industrialisation under Stalin would include: all based on Five-Year Plans, which set out what was going to be produced and also set targets for how much should be produced; industry was also predominantly heavy industry, often in factories built from scratch in places where the state decided they needed to be. Industrialisation was also extremely rapid, involved slave labour to a certain extent via the Gulag prison camp system, and depended also on propaganda-led Stakhanovite efforts. Women were a key part of the workforce, with state provision of childcare to allow this.

27. Industrialisation: successes and failures

Reasons for thinking it was a success include: the increases in production in heavy industry; the increases in production of raw materials; the USSR's ability to eventually defeat Germany in the war of 1941–45; the social mobility (people from peasant or worker backgrounds being promoted into management positions) that resulted from the combination of collectivisation, industrialisation and major education campaigns (together with the purges, which made a lot of managerial positions vacant); the opportunities for women and ethnic minorities that came from industrialisation; the mobilisation of the workforce to make the sacrifices necessary for 'building socialism'.

Reasons for arguing that the industrialisation was not successful could include: the low quality of the products; the inefficiency and wastefulness of the central planning process; the lack of production for consumers; the environmental impacts of so much heavy industrialisation; the reliance in part on the slave labour of the Gulag system; the terribly dangerous working conditions.

Life in the Soviet Union
28. Living and working conditions

The poster includes some interesting details that back up its message of life becoming better for Soviet citizens each day: the woman wears a wristwatch and is standing by a car. She has a medal on her chest, suggesting she has earned these good things by serving the state. She is standing and looking into the future in a field of wheat – representing there being plenty of food for everyone. Electricity pylons represent development of all rural areas of Russia and also industrialisation – this is a modern country. The background shows a busy river with boats taking raw materials to industry but also people having fun on the river.

This might have been an accurate picture for a very small number of party members but for most Soviet citizens life was not very often like this. Very few citizens had cars and if they had wristwatches, they were cheap, badly made and frequently in need of repair. Basic food might have been available but there were not many consumer goods to buy and most urban families relied on relatives in the countryside or their own garden plots for fresh vegetables. Many urban families lived in a single room, often sharing a kitchen and toilet with many other families.

Women and ethnic minorities
29. Changes for women and the family

Answers could include: women were largely excluded from senior positions in the Communist Party and from positions of power in most parts of Soviet life (except in certain parts of the health and education sectors); women were included in working life but were then expected to do all the housework and childcare; women's pay was well below what men were paid for doing the same jobs; women did not have control over their own bodies in terms of abortion being made illegal and contraception being hard to obtain.

30. Persecution of ethnic minorities

Stalin thought that some of the ethnic minorities living within the USSR were enemies of the people, and a threat to the USSR. In some cases – for example, Poles, Germans and Finns – this was because of their ethnic link to countries who shared a border with the USSR. Stalin was also concerned that some ethnic minorities might have counter-revolutionary tendencies.

PRACTICE
40. Practice

1 (i) What I can infer: Stalin said that the Stakhanovites were people who had 'completely mastered' their jobs in every detail. This suggests that Stalin believed, under socialism, workers would be able to become much better at their jobs and more productive, making the USSR better off than capitalist countries.

   Details in the source that tell me this: The information about how much better the Stakhanovites are than the 'engineers, technicians and business executives' who, under capitalism, would be the ones put in charge of increasing productivity. Instead, under socialism, it is the workers themselves who show others how to do this.

   (ii) What I can infer: I can infer that Stalin wanted to encourage more people to become Stakhanovites because he made a speech to a Stakhanovite conference in 1935.

   Details in the source that tell me this: The information about the source and the highly positive way Stakhanovites are described by Stalin. This speech would have been published in Soviet newspapers for everyone to read.

41. Practice

2 There are a number of reasons why the Bolsheviks were able to win the Civil War in 1921. The Red Army was obviously very important as the Bolsheviks' fighting force. It was formed from the Red Guards in January 1918. At first it was a volunteer army, run on socialist lines so that no one was in charge of anyone else. This was a recipe for disaster, but when Trotsky was appointed war commissar in March 1918, he quickly began to transform the Red Army into an effective army. For example, he conscripted lots of former officers from the old tsarist army: 250 000 by 1920. This was important for Bolshevik victory because these men had the skills and experience the old Red Army lacked. In order to make sure they stayed loyal to the

Bolsheviks, Trotsky ordered that the families of the tsarist officers were kept hostage.

Trotsky also introduced brutal discipline to the Red Army, which meant soldiers knew they had no real choice: they had to fight against the White enemy rather than running away, or they would be shot by their own side, or they would get their friends shot. This meant that Red Army soldiers kept fighting even when battles turned against them. This was very important in defending major cities against White attacks. At the same time, Trotsky encouraged Red Army soldiers with a special medal to honour bravery, and with the Socialist Military Oath. These all made the Red Army a more efficient fighting force, which was a cause of the Bolshevik victory.

The Whites had several disadvantages against the Reds which contributed to the Bolshevik victory. For a start there were far fewer Whites than Red Army soldiers: while the Reds had more than 5 million soldiers by 1920, the Whites only had around 250 000. This meant that the Whites were not realistically in a strong position to win the war once Bolshevik conscription into the Red Army was under way. While the Reds controlled central Russia, with its factories and railway network, the Whites were spread out in peripheral areas of Russia, areas without the factories needed for war production.

But perhaps the major cause of White weakness, and therefore of the Bolshevik victory, was that the Whites did not have one single leader to unite opposition against the Bolsheviks. Instead, the different White leaders – Admiral Kolchak in Siberia, General Denikin in Ukraine and southern Russia, General Yudenich in Estonia and the west of Russia – were rivals who competed against each other. Instead of combining their forces, this weakened the Whites and was a major reason for the eventual victory of the Bolsheviks in 1921.

In conclusion, there were many reasons for the Bolshevik victory in the Civil War, including strengths on the Bolshevik side but, just as importantly, weaknesses on the side of the Whites.

44. Practice

3(a) Both Sources B and C are useful for finding out about how ordinary people reacted to the show trials. Source B is useful because it informs us that factory soviets had some sort of role in deciding punishment for show trial victims. The photo shows that the vast majority of people do have their hands raised to vote for the election: probably everyone does.

Source C is useful because this letter suggests that some Soviet citizens felt outraged at the idea of senior Bolsheviks actually spying for fascists from other countries and trying to damage the Soviet Union. The letter also says that honest people should observe everyone they know really carefully in case they were secret followers of Zinoviev and Trotsky, too.

However, there are some drawbacks with both sources for this enquiry. For example, Source B was probably taken for propaganda reasons and it is likely that people in the photo would have understood that if they did not vote for execution then there would be extremely serious consequences for them and their family and friends. Source C may have been what many ordinary people thought about the show trials, but we do not have records from ordinary Soviet citizens to compare it with. It is possible that the writer of Source C wrote in this way in order to get a promotion, or maybe to avoid being put under suspicion themselves.

46. Practice

3(b) Interpretations 1 and 2 both discuss the terror but offer different views about Stalin's role. Interpretation 1 says that Stalin was directly responsible for the terror and that it was Stalin's paranoia that was his motivation for 'launching' political terror, because he wanted to get rid of everyone within the party who he couldn't trust or felt might be a rival.

The central difference in the two interpretations is that Interpretation 2 suggests that Stalin 'sent out signals' that other people picked up on and acted on, so that Stalin did not organise or 'launch' the terror as Interpretation 1 says. For Interpretation 2, Stalin's responsibility is more that he inspired the terror, and was the only one who could have stopped the terror – which he didn't do.

47. Practice

3(c) Interpretations 1 and 2 offer different views because Interpretation 1 is saying that Stalin was directly responsible for the terror and that his paranoia was an important factor in explaining why he launched the terror, while Interpretation 2 sees the terror happening more because the whole of Soviet society went mad, so that it wasn't just Stalin but lots and lots of people who saw 'enemies everywhere'. Interpretation 2 is supported by Source C, written by a Soviet citizen, which suggests the need for all Bolsheviks to spy on their friends.

The main reason why these interpretations offer different views is that the historians have a different focus rather than because they are using different sources or different evidence. Interpretation 1 is interested in how one individual, Stalin, made things happen: the 'cult of Stalin', for example, which meant that Stalin became an almost godlike individual who was able to order the arrest and torture of millions of people without anyone questioning this. Interpretation 2, though, is not so convinced that one person could have been responsible for the terror, despite the cult of Stalin: Lovell, instead, is more interested in the ways in which the society that experienced the terror was also the society that encouraged it and carried it out.

48. Practice

3(d) I agree with the views in Interpretation 1 to quite an extent, because I do not believe that the terror would have happened in the way it did if Stalin had not been paranoid about his political rivals within the party and Stalin had the most to gain from removing any possible challengers to his leadership. Most historians agree that the terror began after the murder of Kirov in December 1934. As a very popular senior communist and leader of the party in Leningrad, Kirov was a serious rival to Stalin and he had also refused to go along with some of Stalin's proposals in the Central Committee. The investigation into Kirov's shooting showed every sign of being a cover-up. Stalin then made his rivals, Zinoviev and Kamenev, the main suspects for Kirov's murder, and the terror began. The terror also had the result that Stalin's rule became unquestioned – people were so terrified of further purges that everyone simply obeyed Stalin. Again, this supports the idea that Stalin was responsible for the terror, because it benefited him and strengthened his position.

However, a limitation of Interpretation 1 is that it does not consider the question that Interpretation 2 raises: how was it that Soviet society went along with the 'madness' of the terror? Although Stalin went on to be a terrifying figure who was never disobeyed, this was not the case before the terror – Kirov and other party bosses had blocked his proposals in 1934, for example. Interpretation 2's viewpoint is very interesting, therefore. Lovell sees Stalin as 'sending out signals' that other people in Soviet society picked up on and acted on: for example, the signal that after Kirov's murder, there must be enemies everywhere. It was not Stalin who arrested innocent people, tortured them into false confessions and then executed them with a shot to the back of the head. But it was Stalin who told Yagoda's replacement as the head of the NKVD that arrests were 'four years' behind where they should be. Since Yagoda had been executed for being too slow in making arrests, Yezhov was strongly incentivised by Stalin's 'signals' to hugely increase the number of people arrested and confessing.

Another limitation of Interpretation 1 is that it does not consider the role of purges in the Civil War, before Stalin became leader. The secret police carried out very similar tactics in rooting out 'enemies of the people' in areas captured from White or other opposition forces: arrests and executions without any proper trial. So although the terror was on a colossal scale, it is possible to say that something similar might have happened if someone else had eventually succeeded Lenin as leader, instead of Stalin. The Bolshevik Party had developed as an underground revolutionary party, constantly under attack from the tsarist police, with party members constantly suspecting each other of being police informers or undercover agents.

However, although Interpretation 2 has many strengths, I do agree with Interpretation 1's analysis because, as Interpretation 2 says, Stalin knew about the scale of the terror and did nothing to stop it. Stalin gave the orders that other people interpreted, so if Stalin had been appalled or even surprised that so many people were being arrested and convicted of being enemies of the people, he could have shut the Terror down or reduced its impact – in the way, for example, that collectivisation was put on hold in 1930 following Stalin's 'dizzy with success' speech. The fact that he did not means, in my view, that he was entirely responsible for the terror.

Notes

Published by Pearson Education Limited, 80 Strand, London, WC2R 0RL.

www.pearsonschoolsandfecolleges.co.uk

Copies of official specifications for all Pearson qualifications may be found on the website: qualifications.pearson.com

Text and illustrations © Pearson Education Ltd 2017
Produced, typeset and illustrated by Tech-Set Ltd.
Cover illustration by Eoin Coveney
Picture research by Alison Prior

The right of Rob Bircher to be identified as author of this work has been asserted by him in accordance with the Copyright, Designs and Patents Act 1988. Content written by Brian Dowse, Victoria Payne and Kirsty Taylor is included.

First published 2017

20 19 18 17

10 9 8 7 6 5 4 3 2 1

British Library Cataloguing in Publication Data

A catalogue record for this book is available from the British Library

ISBN 978 1 292 17643 7

Printed in Slovakia by Neografia

Acknowledgements

Page 5, 20, 21 & 22: Revise Edexcel GCSE History A The Making of the Modern World Revision Guide, Rob Bircher, Copyright © 2015 Pearson Education Inc. All Rights Reserved.

The publisher would like to thank the following for their kind permission to reproduce their photographs:

(Key: b-bottom; c-centre; l-left; r-right; t-top)

Alamy Stock Photo: GL Archive 10, Heritage Image Partnership Ltd 19tl, INTERFOTO 8, 27, Photoresearchers Inc 5t, SPUTNIK 6, 19cl, World History Archive 18; **Bridgeman Art Library Ltd:** The Advertising Archives 28; **Getty Images:** AFP 29, 33, Bettmann 19br, Fotosearch 30, Heritage Images 13, 17, 23, Hulton Archive 5b, Keystone France 39, Print Collector 2, 7l, 7r, Sovfoto 52, SVF2 25, thomas johnson 22, ullsteinbild 4, Underwood Archives 19tr, Universal History Archive 21, 26, Universalimagesgroup 19bl

All other images © Pearson Education

Notes from the publisher

1. In order to ensure that this resource offers high-quality support for the associated Pearson qualification, it has been through a review process by the awarding body. This process confirms that this resource fully covers the teaching and learning content of the specification or part of a specification at which it is aimed. It also confirms that it demonstrates an appropriate balance between the development of subject skills, knowledge and understanding, in addition to preparation for assessment.

Endorsement does not cover any guidance on assessment activities or processes (e.g. practice questions or advice on how to answer assessment questions) included in the resource, nor does it prescribe any particular approach to the teaching or delivery of a related course.

While the publishers have made every attempt to ensure that advice on the qualification and its assessment is accurate, the official specification and associated assessment guidance materials are the only authoritative source of information and should always be referred to for definitive guidance.

Pearson examiners have not contributed to any sections in this resource relevant to examination papers for which they have responsibility.

Endorsement of a resource does not mean that the resource is required to achieve this Pearson qualification, nor does it mean that it is the only suitable material available to support the qualification, and any resource lists produced by the awarding body shall include this and other appropriate resources.

2. Pearson has robust editorial processes, including answer and fact checks, to ensure the accuracy of the content in this publication, and every effort is made to ensure this publication is free of errors. We are, however, only human, and occasionally errors do occur.

Pearson is not liable for any misunderstandings that arise as a result of errors in this publication, but it is our priority to ensure that the content is accurate. If you spot an error, please do contact us at resourcescorrections@pearson.com so we can make sure it is corrected.